Do you get  series: Volume 1

Trust

How to Put it Back In Business

Written By
Todd Welch

In collaboration with Robert Porter Lynch

1/6/10

Lee Ann,

Live Your Truth!

Todd W. Welch

First Edition: 2009
ISBN: 978-0-615-33855-2

Contents

Why it

Whatever path led you here, I am happy you found your way. If you have an entrepreneurial spirit, you and I share a common passion. We're the creative doers, bringing ideas to life. We're the organizers of people. We see opportunities where others see problems. We experiment, fail, and do it all over again, until we succeed, creating jobs and fueling the economy.

In the last two centuries, the American system of free enterprise created an incubator for many of the world's greatest innovations. From this country's garages and kitchens, we've been the beneficiaries of amazing products and services. We owe a debt to the Founding Fathers who established and encouraged the entrepreneurial culture of our country.

The challenge? In this new, global economy not everyone plays by the same rules; corruption is rampant and our enviroment is taking a beating. We face competition from countries working hard to dominate our major industries. Our world is changing faster than we ever imagined. We're confronted by inside forces too, as big government and big business take center stage, while our start-ups and small businesses struggle for survival, against the backdrop of an unpredictable economy. There is a lot of work to be done.

Who is going to fix  ? The same people who always do, us. I am not sure the rest of our country knows it yet, but they need us, and they need us now! Instead of nurturing the next generation of entrepreneurs, our society is more focused on feeding the dinosaurs. We're on our own. We must fend for ourselves, but, in a way, I like the challenge. It keeps us hungry and sharp. I never wanted a hand-out, and I'm always willing to pull my own weight. I suspect you are, too.

What we need is an entrepreneurial approach to entrepreneurship. For over 20 years, my partners and I have tested a new tool called *Cooperative Entrepreneurship (CE)*. We've only scratched the surface of CE's capabilities. We believe CE can build a culture that will foster even greater and more prolific innovations. The future lies not with one genius in a garage, but in connecting the garages into networks of trusted peers innovating together.

I'll share much of what we've learned about Cooperative Entrepreneurship through real-world stories. Many of these stories will be complemented by related data and other resources to give you as clear a picture as possible.

We'll start with the story of my family's business in the 1980s and the birth of Cooperative Entrepreneurship. This love of entrepreneurship started around my family's dinner table and extended naturally into our work. Dad built a leading insurance agency; Mom operated a children's clothing business; my sister Jody created a children's day care center, and I partnered with my brother Glen to start a company called Charter Partners. Charter Partners has been the proving ground for Cooperative Entrepreneurship. By implementing CE's principles with over 300 companies, we've seen its positive benefits firsthand.

When we speak of entrepreneurship, we're talking about each individual person's ability to innovate in the broadest sense, not just those that create "business." Entrepreneurs exist in both large and small companies. A commonly held belief is that big business has the benefit of leverage, stability, and knowledge. Small businesses have the benefits of trust, flexibility, and creativity. Cooperative Entrepreneurship allows both to enjoy the benefits of the other.

Cooperative Entrepreneurship starts with a decision to adopt new thinking that everyone in your network can use to improve the speed, quantity, and quality of innovation. This includes your employees, suppliers, customers, advisors and believe it or not . . . even competitors. With this book, I intend to extend our 20-year experiment into the minds and hearts of many and do nothing less than reinvent *entrepreneurship* itself.

One more thing...I am still learning to live 🔵 myself because I know I can do better, I also know the world can be different because *we* can do better. If you feel a little fuzzy about what 🔵 is, don't concern yourself. I am confident that the further you journey into this book the more clear the answer will become. I enjoyed writing this for you and I hope you will enjoy the experience.

Todd Welch

Before it

1

After 20 years in business, our family insurance agency, Bowers, Schumann and Welch (BS&W), developed a reputation — our clients trusted us. We were ranked as one of America's top 100 brokers. Nearly three out of four small businesses, non-profits, and government organizations in our region were insured through our family business, an unbelievable market penetration.

With this level of success, I've always felt a sense of pride being part of the Welch family. My dad, Scott Welch, grew up in a working-class family, and he knew how to bring people together. With five younger brothers, he had plenty of practice, but that was not the type of business world he joined as a young, hungry, insurance broker. He joined the world of "beat the competition," and he was good at it. While most insurance agents sat in their offices waiting for someone to walk in, Dad was out on the street, wearing out his shoe leather with the mantra, "You might as well give in now, because sooner or later you'll be insured with me." Several years after he started, Dad did just that. The competition was dwarfed by comparison. He learned that by building volume with the insurance companies, it gave him more control. He had to be big to have clout. Dad found a way to build a winning organization and he did it honorably.

There was a famous story that was told over and over at BS&W. In the early years of BS&W, a client came into the office to report an accident. His small truck was declared a total loss. There were only a few employees at the time and Dad was documenting the claim for him. He realized a mistake was made in the original application and the customer had no coverage for his truck.

He hadn't faced this situation before and felt anxious. What should he do? He excused himself to have a private consultation with his senior partner, Leonard Schumann. After listening to Dad's story, Leonard said, "Well Scott, I'm not sure what we are going to do, but I am sure that it starts with telling him the truth." Afterwards, everyone at BS&W knew our values and clearly what to do if they got into a similar situation.

Dad was also the consummate, community-minded citizen. He spent time helping develop local programs to support the Kiwanis, Boy Scouts, and police department. He sat on the founding boards for our community college, retirement village, and a domestic abuse shelter. Because of his involvement, he was well liked and respected. Many times, Dad was asked to run for political office.

Then, in March 1986, a crisis jeopardized everything he had worked so hard to create. The cover of *Time* [1] read:

Our clients were in financial crisis and some were blaming our family business

Question:

What do you do in a crisis?

As the crisis picked up, public schools, one of our key business segments, were hit hard. Insurance rates were raised many times the cost of previous years or policies were unavailable at any price.

In board meeting after board meeting, I watched my father defend why the rates had gone up so dramatically. The outcome of intense competition, high interest rates, and overzealous investment between the insurance companies created the crisis. No one in our region, including Dad, had any control over these events. However, BS&W and the Welch family name continued to be in the newspaper and associated with unreasonable insurance rate increases. Public officials threatened to resign due to loss of

---

[1] Printed with permission Wright's reprints

liability coverage, and budgets were busted. The communities' anger and frustration boiled over.

Just when most people would run for the hills, Dad did the unexpected: he invited every frustrated public authority to a joint conference at our office. On the surface, you might think him crazy. There was some real tension in the room as the meeting convened. I watched as Dad facilitated a meeting that encouraged everyone to vent their fears, gave the group tools to educate themselves about the facts, and allowed the group to create a future. Amazingly, he moved them from crisis to creativity, discovering their own answer along the way. In my view, he went from zero to hero, and it left an indelible impression on me.

As the school group built their confidence in the facts surrounding their situation, they also built trust with each other. They now had the ability to determine their own future, and they did exactly that. Fourteen public schools came together to form the Warren Hunterdon Insurance Pool (WHIP). WHIP became so successful that two adjoining counties in New Jersey, Morris, and Sussex, asked to join.

The cooperative partnership grew, and several hundred schools are now involved in the pool. Insurance rates stabilized, and the self-insurance fund they created, starting at $5 million, is now worth over $100 million—a true success story.

However, there were learning experiences along the way. For example, some schools "excused themselves" from participating. Later, we found choosing not to participate was a key element of group formation. Some people and groups don't fit the collaboration mold or current standards and politely leave. To our surprise, this consolidation made the core group even stronger.

Question:

Can this model apply to business?

This experience was an awakening for me, it changed my life. I started to think about my passion for entrepreneurship and wondered if I could bring our business clients together and help them to build new products for themselves. By encouraging collaboration between similar businesses, they could gain the benefits of a company ten times their size. These thoughts were the seeds that grew into Cooperative Entrepreneurship.

When I suggested promoting the new innovation model to businesses, my father and Glen said, "It can't be done." They believed it was the non-profit component that allowed the schools and municipalities to work together, and direct competitors would not adopt it. So, what happens when you're told by your brother and father something can't be done? You have to prove them wrong! The gauntlet was thrown down, and I had to take the risk.

I started by looking for what I call an "un-market," an underserved audience. In our area, this un-market was the Waste and Septic Haulers (WASH). Here's a group only a mother could love. These are the toughest guys in the business, and everyone knew they'd never work together. Working together meant running against a long history of deep competition. I searched for an insider, someone to teach me the ropes and help me identify the most respected businesses in the industry.

I found a few organizations interested in hearing about our concept including Russell Reid, the largest and most respected waste contractor in our area. I continued looking for similar organizations to form a group of peers. My first step was organizing a meeting to share the WHIP experience and the collaboration model. At the opening meeting, things seemed to go well.

The prospective members sat quietly in a U-shaped conference room. I started with our Pre-Meeting Statement, clarifying that our model wasn't collusion, price fixing or restraint of trade. Our goals were to reduce costs, increase sales, and innovate. I told the story of WHIP and the possibilities of collaboration. At the end of the presentation, I hoped for a round of applause and a healthy group discussion.

Instead, a gentleman to my left stood up, pointed to another fellow across the table and exclaimed, "That SOB's father firebombed one of our trucks in 1955, and I'll be damned if I will sit in the same room as him!"

My first thought was, "Dad and Glen were right."

I quickly realized two things were missing. First, there was no common culture to ease their communication. Second, I selected the attendees without understanding the inter-relationships. When I asked the contractors to select their own peer team members, the group formed quickly and peacefully. Peers are critical to the success of the group.

In subsequent meetings, the group identified common needs, and members solved each other's problems. For example, a member offered their Human Resource policies to another who did not have policies in place. *Coopetition* was born. Now we were creating a common language and culture to strengthen the group's bond.

Question:

What is the right size for an alliance?

After our success with WASH, we formed a building contractors group that started with three members and quickly grew to over 90. As it grew, the group became more of an association than a close, peer network. They lost the feeling of being connected and the level of trust it brings. The group's size made it difficult to build personal relationships or communicate on a partnership level. We started to get caught up in awards, ceremonies and networking events.

From this experience we learned that smaller groups with personal relationships were key to innovation.

In practice, we form groups as small as 3 and as large as 20. Groups of many sizes can work.

Then we discovered some interesting facts that help support why we feel 12 is the best group size for us. There are:

12 inches in a foot
12 months in a year
12 jurors for a trial
12 function keys on a keyboard
12 buttons on a phone
12 hues in a color wheel
12 signs in the zodiac
12 ribs in the human body
12 hours on a clock
12 grades in judo
12 donuts in a dozen
12 men walked on the moon

With facts like these, who were we to fight the trend?

Question:

How do you keep a group from stagnating?

Walt Disney is a hero for my entire family. So when Mike Vance, who spent years in charge of idea and people development for Walt Disney, was scheduled to speak on innovation and creativity Glen and I decided to attend. During the seminar, Mike told one amazing Walt Disney story after the other.

One story stood out. Walt Disney constantly reinvented the Disney Company, or as Mike called it repotting. We know that innovation is now the de facto standard for growth. Mike put forth the idea that when you or an

> Ships are designed to leave port.

organization grows, you can get root bound like a plant that's outgrown its pot. When a plant becomes root bound it dies. The same applies for the human spirit and company strategies. He suggested people and businesses must constantly monitor their progress, and when necessary, get a new pot, new style, new strategy, new people, and new ideas.

Back home, we presented our repotting idea to Dad, the Development Center. A satellite facility, the Development Center was a place where we could build a future for our family business. We were taking a risk. No one could imagine an insurance research and development center. The insurance business hadn't changed much in the last 350 years. What were we going to discover?

New ideas were colliding with old, but we knew that bringing divergent thinking together created an opportunity for a new vision. For whatever crazy reason, Dad supported our repotting, gave us a budget, and a one-year deadline.

We were learning fast and enjoying it, too, so much that we got an extension, and one year turned into three. During this time, we met key industry players. We gained a broader view of the challenges and opportunities the industry faced. More people inquired about our efforts, and a buzz started. We started feeling pressure to share our findings.

We were frustrated. We had great insight into the industry's challenges; we had great new relationships, but no clear idea of a holistic solution to the problems we were seeing. We spent untold hours researching, thinking, and sorting through masses of data. Our work room looked like a research lab with papers on the walls and detailed math problems on the board. However, we hadn't yet reached our version of $E=MC^2$. Where was our simple answer to the complex problems of our industry? That's when Dad swung open the door of the work room and announced, "I GOT IT."

When we asked, "What?" Dad picked up a marker, wrote down one word, and pinned it on the idea board.

Lessons Learned:

1. There is a new way to compete called Cooperative Entrepreneurship.

2. You can turn adversity into opportunity if you are willing to listen.

3. Trusting in your clients to help solve their own problems takes courage.

4. Successful groups are peer selected and establish a common culture.

5. When peers trust each other, they will share best practices and help each other solve common problems.

6. When groups are too small, energy is missing, and when too large, people feel disconnected.

7. Don't firebomb your competitors' equipment; it really makes them mad for a very long time.

Discovery of it 2

Trust? Dad was excited. Glen and I wanted to be excited, too. But frankly, we were thinking, "Trust?" It's a nice concept, but hasn't corruption been around since the beginning of time? If we can fix corruption we might as well work on world hunger and global warming.

Dad reminded us that everything we were learning pointed to a breakdown of trust in the insurance system. The existing system built in massive frictional costs to protect people from each other. He said our challenge was to build a system that put trust back in the equation. If we did, think of the possibilities.

What Dad said started to make sense, but we didn't know where to start. We faced a new journey of discovery. We began by looking for ideas and tools to help us learn about trust.

Next stop Ojai, California.

Question:

How do you make trust tangible?

The idea for the Trust Towel started during a leadership conference in sunny California. To get things started, a beanbag was tossed around, encouraging attendees to speak out about their experiences when they caught it. The group seemed to enjoy using this tool.

Over dinner that evening, we were seated with the management team of a manufacturing company. We had been discussing, in general terms, a difficult problem involving a key employee. Suggestions were tossed about until the CEO of the manufacturing firm picked up his napkin, tossed it onto the center of the table, and said, "Tell him the truth; just be honest!" Everyone at the table knew he was right and that's exactly what we did. We followed his advice, it was difficult conversation, but it was the best for both us and the employee.

Glen and I started thinking about ways that we could co-create something tangible that would remind people about the importance of truth in our culture. We drew a picture of a bull stamped with the universal no symbol, a circle with a diagonal. Now that we had our "NO Bull," we needed to tie it to something you could toss around if someone violated the NO Bull rule during one of our group meetings. We put the bull symbol on a towel and the Trust Towel was born. After presenting the towel at an alliance meeting of the WASH Group, the members immediately adopted it.

The Trust Towel reached iconic status as a symbol for the values we embrace. Over the years, five additional symbols have been added, representing important aspects of our culture. The Trust Towel's six rules help us build common values with our partner companies.

NO BULL. Tell the truth. Lies create cracks in the foundation of all relationships. When people commit to honor and integrity, trust prospers.

 NO DISRESPECT. Be Respectful. Put downs, interruptions, insults and inattention are all trust busters. Mutual respect is the path to building trust.

 NO BACK STABBING. Talk to people not about people. Betrayal is among the worst of all human behaviors. When something needs to be said, say it to that person.

 NO WHINING. Be Positive. Negative energy, destroys security and hope. State the problem then begin working on the solution.

 NO SURPRISES. Partners don't surprise partners. Bad surprises, ruin relationships. Communication builds mutual understanding.

 NO WASTING TIME. Respect other people's time. There is nothing more valuable than time. When someone offers you theirs, spend it wisely.

Our members developed rules around what happens when you violate one of the tenets.

1. You "get the towel," tossed at you for a violation.

2. If you are guilty, you donate $1 to the Trust Bucket and the money collected over the year is given to a charity (we have collected as much as $2,500 in fines a year).

Since the Trust Towel was first introduced, we have printed over 10,000. It's popularity is primarily due to how the Trust Towel makes trust fun! We have found that 90% of trust violations, during our meetings, come from putdowns. Interestingly, we found when people trust each other they tend to tease each other more, and they laugh more. These rules are a great tool to get people to build trust constructively. As an example, some of our more entertaining members come into the room and put a $20 bill in the bucket saying, "OK, lets get started!"

Question:

How much does trust cost?

Our next stop was a presentation to 500 insurance professionals in Scottsdale, Arizona. Maurice "Hank" Greenberg, the past chairman of AIG, was the speaker before us. At the time, AIG was known as an aggressive, investor-focused, mega-corporation with shrewd, talented people. Following Greenberg's presentation made talking about trust feel even more difficult. After Hank shared his view of the future, we spoke about markedly different concepts—coopetition, partnership, long-term relationships, honesty, and collaboration. The polite, but less than enthusiastic, response left us thinking our view had hardly been heard.

Several years later, AIG took center stage in a worldwide, economic meltdown. Imagine if we had concluded our presentation by saying, "No matter your intelligence, no matter how hard you work, and no matter how powerful you are, in the near future, 30-50% of your wealth will evaporate almost overnight unless we pay attention to this 5 letter word, trust." Maybe there is something to trust after all.

After California and Arizona, we began to understand the insurance system was broken. We knew if we could bring trust back, we could save billions of dollars, reducing policy holder costs and increasing company profits.

Consider an example from the Commercial Property and Casualty Insurance business:

- Forty percent of customers had fled standard insurers.

- An annual churn rate of 25% among the customer base was the norm.

- For 15 years, the industry did not make a profit on the underwriting side of the business.

- Almost no policies were delivered error free.

- No one was satisfied.

We concluded fine tuning the insurance system wouldn't fix the problem. We needed a massive shift in thinking and structure, a new model. We drew a picture of the relationship in the value chain with the frictional costs included and eliminated. We did an analysis to see what a premium dollar could "buy" in a collaborative system versus the current adversarial system. The numbers were astounding. So great was the difference we were worried no one would believe you could find an extra 25¢ in every premium dollar. *Nearly all the savings related to a lack of trust in the system.*

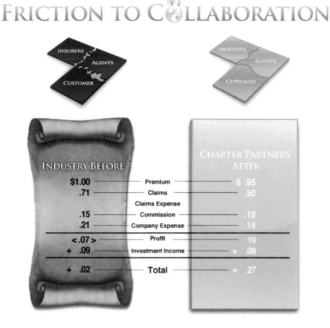

Question:

How do you change an industry?

Our next step was to host a meeting for the presidents of America's leading insurance companies. We believed we had discovered a way to impact dramatically the frictional industry costs. Cooperative Entrepreneurship could give these leaders everything they wanted: more profit, loyal customers, and expanded revenue. Once the presidents saw the data and discussed ways to make change happen, we might have a chance to make change a reality.

How do you organize a meeting of this magnitude? At first, we were intimidated by our own idea. What are we going to do with them when they get here and how do we get them here in the first place?

We started by setting a clear agenda worthy of the people attending. The message we needed to deliver was about trust. Even though our industry was based on trust, we wondered who would show up to talk about it. How do we get them to attend? A brochure or an e-mail wouldn't work. These were successful, respected executives. We searched for the best way to connect. Since peer invitation had worked for our entrepreneurial groups, we believed it might work for this group also.

We did not have enough relationship equity to make a personal invitation to all the presidents, but we did have it with a few. We started with a president we'd known for a number of years, explaining the meeting's focus and our goal to have industry presidents attend. He liked the idea and helped us refine the agenda and the invitation list.

We started with one and jointly invited two other presidents who agreed to attend. They helped us select other candidates. Using this method, we were introduced to people we never would meet otherwise. The meeting evolved into a full house of industry leaders. They were coming not only because they were interested in the topic, but because they were also interested in spending time with each other. As a result of this experience, peer invitations have become the standard way we like to form new alliances.

The meeting was a success, but things didn't work out exactly as planned. Our ideas, albeit not fully developed, were ahead of their time. Instead of changing the industry, we changed ourselves and our family business. The other good news? We learned more about developing alliances. Many of the relationships we created were bridges that helped us achieve our current success. Most importantly, we developed a new level of confidence. We were more committed than ever to Cooperative Entrepreneurship.

Money Saving Tip: If you ever decide to host the presidents of America's insurance companies at your office, remember that your lawn maintenance guy is on the team too. After bringing together what is likely the most influential group of people ever assembled in Washington, New Jersey, we kicked off the meeting to the deafening whine of a weed-whacker. I remember the look on my team members' faces as they realized what was happening. A few moved to the door to stop the impending doom. The next few minutes were completely drowned out by the revving of the two-stroke engine just outside the window. With that many highly paid people sitting idle while we waited for the noise to stop, I wondered what the real cost was for not including him in the game-plan.

Talking with our landscaper after the meeting, he suggested not only notifying him, but letting him be part of the team. He had some ideas about making the event better. He said that plants and color can set a mood, and if given the opportunity, he could set up a visual experience at the building entrance that impacts meeting attendees and improves their experience. Our conversation reminded me to include everyone on the team—even the less obvious—because everyone can be entrepreneurial!

The journey continued as we formed more Cooperative Entrepreneurship Alliances (CEAs). We formed CEAs at a steady rate: long-haul truckers, real estate owners, HVAC companies, building supply companies, manufacturers, school bus operators, doctors, golf courses and fuel oil dealers. Our biggest success came when we created a Captive insurance company owned by the members.

Question:

What is the definition of a champion?

Every alliance starts with a champion, someone to lead the way into the future. Gino Nicolai of Hannabery HVAC, was a champion's champion. Gino came with the reputation of being a leading entrepreneur with a big heart. Gino managed approximately 200 employees and built one of the most successful HVAC companies in the region known for its honesty and quality. It did not take much to get Gino talking about the future. He relayed the following story to me.

A few years earlier, a utility consolidator acquiring HVAC companies requested a meeting with Gino. He agreed and invited his attorney and accountant since he expected a purchase offer. Prior to the meeting, he informed them he did not want to sell.

The consolidator presented a proposal to buy Hannabery HVAC. Gino was also given a warning that if he did not sell, they'd put him out of business.

> **Champions are a precious resource.**
>
> Rule #1: Never mistreat an advocate.
> - Scott Welch

Like many entrepreneurs, Gino got into business to gain some control over his life. He loved his work and felt responsible for his employees. What he heard was a threat not only to his way of life, but also to theirs.

After some thought, Gino asked his most respected peers (even competitors) to meet for lunch. He described the consolidator's proposal and warning, knowing that these other businesses would be approached next. Gino proposed an alternative to selling to benefit them all.

He suggested creating an alliance, one that allows each member to remain independent but also helps them become stronger. As Gino put it, "Any business trying to do the right thing, in the right way, is a friend of mine. Anyone who is cheating, being dishonest, or practicing less than optimal integrity, they're my enemies. These guys are not our friends."

To describe the group's strength, he compared it to breaking one stick at a time, an easy task. Once you bundle a group of sticks together, however, it can be impossible to break.

Gino and his peers formed the Independent Quality Alliance. As a team they purchase supplies, share leads, and partnered with a college to educate employees on best practices. Best of all, everyone from the customers to the owners were benefited from the alliance. Gino said it best, "What else are you supposed to do in business? If everybody wins, it's a great situation."

Gino challenged us to expand our alliance. "We can do more than just insurance since we have established a bond," Gino said. "Why not allow everyone to share ideas and resources?" Gino wanted us to repot ourselves. Sadly, Gino passed away shortly after sharing his wisdom. Out of respect for his leadership,

Charter Partners created the Gino Nicolai Partner of the Year award.

The Power of it

We considered Gino's challenge, and in 2002, we proposed his idea to the entire community at our annual alliance meeting. After a number of storyboard sessions, we looked at the collective economic power of the current members. Measured as a whole, it was in the billions; the alliance would be a top-10 regional employer.

Burn the Ships

July 1519, Spanish conquistador Hermán Cortés orders his men to burn the ships behind them as they go to war in Veracruz, Mexico. There was no retreat; either win or die.

After 33 years as an insurance agency, we had our own burning of the ships. We recognized that if we wanted to put **trust** back into business, we had to give up the old ways, and form a new organization, Charter Partners, to facilitate alliances.

When trying to create something new, I have observed three phases that groups travel through. I call it the three F's, FEAR, FACTS and FUTURE. Gino's suggestion created a level of *fear*, but as we gathered *facts* the fear dissipated, and a number of innovations for the *future* were suggested in key areas like health care, recruiting, and energy. The mold was set, although it would take a number of years for the cooperative to become a reality.

Question:

What's in a Logo?

We shared Gino's story of "breaking the sticks" with our marketing people while they developed the Charter Partners logo. They suggested that our approach sounded like a banyan tree, which grows multiple trunks. They weave together, and from a distance, you think you're seeing a single, large trunk supporting an enormous canopy. In India, they call it the commerce tree because merchants stop to sell their goods under its protective shade.

For our logo, we liked the symbolism of the banyan tree. The leaves (Think) represent the new ideas that come from working in collaboration, the trunk (Team) symbolizes our team alliances, and the small seed at the bottom, the red dot, represents integrity and (Trust).

CHARTER
PARTNERS.
The Power of Shared Knowledge ®

Question:

What do you do when someone betrays you?

In the spirit of integrity and trust, I want you to know that everything we tried did not work. In addition to our successes, we failed too, and we paid a price, sometimes a big price. Trust comes with the risk of betrayal. Sometimes we failed to see a partnership's true colors. I share these betrayals and failures with you now, recognizing that you may pass judgment about me and my team. I trust more good can from the honesty.

Betrayal #1

Charter Partners learned how to create a member-owned mutual insurance company and found a reinsurance partner (companies that insure insurance companies) with a strong, passionate team. However, a speculative investment buyer purchased our partner reinsurer. The management team changed, and with it, so did their commitment to our project. The financial crisis following 9-11 created more uncertainty in the industry.

Ostrich Trust
When things get scary you put your head in the sand, pretending it doesn't exist and hide until it's all over.

Shortly thereafter, our reinsurance partner was sold again. Charter Partners was losing its internal advocates, and we didn't realize we were approaching a crisis moment. The new reinsurance owners changed their strategy, and our collaborative relationship did not fit the mold. They started squeezing our alliance members and us until we were out of options. During this time, the reinsurer violated all six rules of the Trust Towel.

We had invested years building trust between 300 independent businesses that agreed to jointly invest in their own mutual insurance company. The reinsurer made a series of changes that added up to a big problem for our company. Eventually, the reinsurer pulled out of the relationship altogether. We were left to find a new partner quickly, but not before many of our members were forced to find alternatives. The reinsurer did not get it and we had an very expensive lesson in trusted partnerships.

Betrayal No. 2

When threatened, fear brings out the true character of companies and individuals. After the reinsurer told us they were not going to honor their agreement, our insurance agent partners, who were distributors of our products needed to preserve their business. It was a time when we needed each other the most. It was a time to pull together. One of the largest agents entered into a secret agreement for his own benefit. The worst part was how the agent manipulated the truth to us and our

Survivor Trust
Instead of working together,
your partner takes the last of the water.

mutual clients This was betrayal on top of betrayal. A partner enjoys a special relationship, and unexpected or unjustified behavior cuts deepest. This betrayal of trust was more hurtful to our organization than the original. Make no mistake about it, it was not "just business," it was personal. The situation brought to mind being stranded on an island and one person drinking all the water while the others are not looking. They did not get it.

Betrayal No. 3

The prior betrayals were bad, but after a 30-year relationship, we were stunned to learn our bank was next in line. The two previous betrayals had a significant and immediate impact on our revenues. After hundreds of millions of dollars in transactions, we anticipated our bank would work with us as we worked through our new financial reality. Our bank representative was in the National Guard and was recently deployed, leaving us with no significant internal advocate. Once the bank saw a dip in our revenue, we were out without any conversation or appeal process. All communication took place via the attorney assigned to our disengagement. We thought we were in a long-term relationship. They thought we were lunch. This third betrayal put us into a deeper financial crisis. It was three hits in a row, and it put our leadership to the test.

Black Widow Trust
Sometimes after mating a female Black Widow spider will eat her mate.

Acknowledging Our Role

Ultimately, we overcame this adversity, but we also realize we bear some responsibility for each of these betrayals. We had warnings about each situation and did not heed them. In the first betrayal, the insurance company was making things difficult for us well before the relationship ended. We didn't pay enough attention to their signals. In the second betrayal, our partners had a history of marginal behavior, and we knew it. In the final betrayal, we surprised our banker with bad

> There is something disconcerting about the fact that we can map the human genome and land a robot on Mars, but we still can't say for sure whether someone is trying to pull the wool over our eyes.
>
> Dina Temple-Raston, NPR

news, breaking our own Trust Towel rule. These mistakes cost us millions. They were painful lessons, and we share them so that you can avoid them. We learned a great deal about trust, and these experiences made us value it even more. What happened didn't change our position on trust. It made us more determined to have better partnerships and to insulate ourselves from those who don't share our values. The more partnerships in the network, the more powerful and secure it becomes. The more networks like ours that form, the less tolerance the world will have for betrayal. We survived and are stronger for the experience. Our betrayers didn't get it either.

Question:

What is the definition of a partner?

A letter from Al Van Riper:

> "Dear Todd, Glen . . . and "the team":
>
> First of all, I don't think you have any idea how much your respect means to me. I am truly honored (and shocked) to be given the "Gino Award." Thank you.
>
> I've been awake all night trying to figure out how to express my feelings of gratitude.
>
> I've always looked forward to our meetings; I've learned so much, and my business has benefited. I have become a better businessman and a better person for it.
>
> After thinking all night I came to the conclusion that the **Perfect Partnership** is when you feel you can never say, "You're welcome," when the other party thanks you. "You're welcome," infers an acknowledgment that you did something to be thanked for and that you didn't benefit greater. Our relationship has had one constant—we both keep sincerely saying, "No, it's **I** who should be thanking **you**."
>
> I leave every meeting, phone conference, and gathering with the same feeling: what do they keep thanking me for? How do I thank these guys for all they've done for me?

Maybe that's the key. Maybe that's the glue — just like in a good marriage. You always feel you're the lucky one. (Why does she stay with me? When is she finally going to figure out that I got the better deal and leave me?) Maybe, just maybe, the measure of a man doesn't always have to be in dollars and cents. Maybe it's in the friendships we build along the way.

I was truly moved. I'm a sappy guy. You almost made me cry in front of 150 people. The payback is I'll never let you say the last thank you.

I THANK YOU ALL.

Your partner, Al

Al gets ⓘ, he raises the bar on trust for all of us. We learned another lesson from Al. If we wanted someone of his quality at a peer meeting, we needed to ensure they really were peers. In past meetings, once the group reached agreement on a key decision, Al stepped up and said, "I'm in." Others responded with, "I'm not authorized to make that decision. I have to go back and check with the boss." This was unfair to Al and disrespectful of his time (Trust Towel rules). Going forward, we made a commitment to ensure only peer decision makers attended future meetings.

Question:

Where is Charter Partners today?

Charter Partners has settled into the role of *faciligrator*. It's a smash-up word, a combination of the words facilitate and integrate (FACILI-GRATE). It means to ease the integration of people, products, and services. A faciligrator serves as a key resource for our members by integrating them into an innovation machine. They are the educator, conductor, stimulator, and administrator providing just in time resources.

Entrepreneurs often believe the task of getting together with peers and innovating is something they should be able to do independently. It also seems obvious that a group of talented entrepreneurs could handle the seemingly minor task of administering themselves. However, this can sometimes end badly.

Not using a faciligrator is like running a football team without a coach, an orchestra without the conductor, or an airport without air traffic control. Chaos ensues. Critical to the team's well being, the faciligrator's role can mean the difference between success and failure.

Charter Partners: The Facts

Charter Partners has successfully created many Cooperative Entrepreneurship Alliances (CEAs). Currently, we collaborate with over 100 independent businesses in our network. These businesses represent 4000+ employees, $650,000,000 in sales, and operation in 18 states, with most in New Jersey and Pennsylvania. Our CEAs are organized around industry groups like manufacturers, transportation, contractors, distributors, professional service providers, and retail companies. These business owners have high standards and care about their employees and communities. Each group works on problem solving, best practices, and ideas for collaboration, including joint ventures.

> **OUR CHARTER**
>
> *We believe privately held entrepreneurial businesses represent the spirit and strength of America. We are committed to creating an environment of mutual trust and respect that attracts groups of quality entrepreneurs who share ideas, products and services to amplify their success.*
>
> *-- The Charter Partners Team*

Community Purchasing Alliance

One benefit of membership is access to the Charter Partners Purchasing Alliance. By working directly with our business owners, we can identify products and services that serve the entire network and improve their business operations. Products and services must come with a member's personal recommendation to be

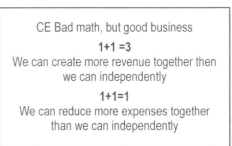

presented to the larger group. Companies that successfully join the purchasing alliance as a supplier understand the value the aggregated group provides, and price accordingly.

Our top three cost reducing products are:

1. Insurance
2. Credit card processing services
3. Wireless communications

Enhancing Courage

My brother Glen often reminds me that the Cooperative Entrepreneurship Alliances also provide an important and often overlooked resource, courage. An entrepreneur is often described as someone with the courage to take risks, to step out on their own, and to give it a go. When you're an entrepreneur, courage gets the process started, but it's also needed day in and day out. As the members build confidence and trust with their peers, they are willing to take more risk together. We're excited to see a group push through competitive concerns to become partners for the benefit of each other. Over and over, we've seen this happen with amazing, bottom-line results.

One of Charter Partner's proudest moments came when the various industry groups came together to form a mutual insurance company. Following an individual decision by company, and a collective decision by peer industry group, 13 groups agreed to form the company. They reminded me of the 13 colonies coming together to form the USA. Risk existed then, as it does now, and each peer group agreed to share the risk as a larger pool overseen by the Board of Directors, demonstrating the value of the broader alliance and its ability to absorb risk.

Each peer group has industry expertise, but because each company can suffer individual catastrophic events, the mutual insurance company allows the risk to be spread out for an ideal scenario. When we combined the power of the 13 groups, with the trust created between the members, we could squeeze out waste, increase profits, and provide stability in a product that directly impacted their bottom lines.

The Charter Partners management team is led by my brother Glen, Vice President, Pattie Cowley, and Director of Insurance Operations, Suzie Stark. They have been together for 20 years and developed the mantra, "The Power of Shared Knowledge." This knowledge resource provided by the members of the alliance in the application of Cooperative Entrepreneurship allows our members to buy better, sell smarter, and innovate faster.

Question:

What can CE do for you?

Tom Kardish, a member of Charter Partners and owner of Doylestown Lumber and Mill Works explains the value of CE:

> Life can be very tough for a small to mid-sized business owner, and it can be very lonely.
>
> The amazing thing about Charter Partners isn't the fact that all these companies came together to do business, but that we genuinely care about each other.
>
> In my situation, I have been trying to buy out a partner for two years. It's difficult to find someone to lend $6 million to any business these days, let alone a lumberyard. Despite a solid niche business, on prime real estate, the constant rejections got me down. Who could I talk to? Well, your fellow business owners that's who.
>
> Charter Partners holds alliance meetings with peer owners of other small businesses. This secure group creates an atmosphere of trust that allowed the sharing of financials, options, hopes, dreams,

motivations, and fears. Though with any intervention, the end result is up to me. Final chapters have yet to be written, but if nothing else, I feel better about trying to push the big rock up the hill. In the end, I know that **Cooperative Entrepreneurship makes me a better person.**

Question:

What about the next generation?

We created the Charter Partners Institute[2], a non-profit organization, to further learning about Cooperative Entrepreneurship. The Institute conducts summer entrepreneurship camps at Charter Farms[3], helping schools create student-led programs and educating teachers who want to shift to this new model of learning.

I had the honor to sit down with Pete Moses the CEO of the Children's Aid Society, the largest and oldest non-profit in New York City. Pete has a better perspective on young people than anyone I have ever met. Pete opened my eyes to the realities facing the younger generation. For instance,

Our greatest natural resource is the minds of our children.

Walter Elias Disney

Pete shared that in New York City, 29% of kids live below the poverty line, despite being the richest city in the world. Even more stunning, 50% of the city's kids do not graduate high school. Fifty percent means 100,000 students a year drop out and can't participate in the new economy.

A reality since the 70s, Pete thinks we're sitting on a powder keg with the fuse lit. Why do so many kids fail to graduate? Why

---

[2] Not-for-profit 501(c)3 .(www.charterpartners.org)

[3] Private corporate retreat for Cooperative Entrepreneurs

are we failing our children? New York City, according to Pete, chooses not to see the big picture, narrowing its view to test taking in English, math, and science. These skills only get you in the game. Skills like responsibility, creativity, and team building give a broader range of life opportunities.

Like a smoking habit, Pete believes society thinks it can get away with ignoring the problem, but at some point, there will be consequences. We share the opinion that fixing the problem will require a community-wide effort. Pete and I hold out hope that more businesses will invest in training young people, seeing it as a ROI for the next decade.

As Charter Partners better understood the value and process of Cooperative Entrepreneurship, a question arose. Can we teach the next generation about Cooperative Entrepreneurship while they are still in school, and if we did, what impact would this have on our society?

I know it would have helped me. I was an average student, often frustrated with the teacher as the "sage-on-the-stage" experience. Like a large water pitcher, teachers expected me to hold all the knowledge they poured into me. How well I poured it back into them determined my grade. Time and again I wondered, "Why am I memorizing all this stuff?"

I did not understand how I could apply all this information to my life. I did what I had to do, but I checked out mentally and tried to find something else of interest. When I entered the business world, the light came on. I became a learning sponge and realized I had talents that weren't acknowledged in high school. No one ever graded me on my ability to lead a team, my honesty, or my creativity. My paycheck was now based on these skills.

In 1993, I approached the principal of Warren Hills High School in Washington, New Jersey, about starting a new program. This program would help kids discover their individual talents, skills useful in the real world, with the goal of getting them excited about their futures. He pointed out that students have opportunities to learn about business and free enterprise through existing programs like Junior Achievement and Future Business Leaders of America.

I responded that those are valuable experiences, but I wanted to run a real "live" business with real money. He said, "I have no budget, but if you can get a teacher to work for free in an after-school program, go ahead."

The principal arranged for me to speak to all the teachers during one of their group meetings. Most just checked their watches, but two, Al Bowan and Ralph Fiore, approached me afterward. They said if I could convince six or more students to join, they would teach the program. Fortunately, a subsequent talk managed to recruit six students willing to give it a try.

At our first meeting we arranged the desks into a circle, so we could face each other, and started brainstorming ideas about what business to start. I asked them to define the biggest challenge they faced and to tell me what they love to do. They lamented how the area offered nothing to do after school and discussed starting a miniature golf course. When they discovered that no one knew much about golf, and it would take intensive capital to start, the conversation turned to babysitting. A much-needed service in the area, babysitting was scrapped when they identified concerns about liability and being sued. Finally, they talked about the low energy level at school in the morning. Kids had a hard time waking up for class. The group also spoke about their love of music. My ears perked up. I heard a real problem, and I heard the word love.

Within a few weeks, the group met weekly, and soon daily, after school. They got permission from the school board, principal, and administration to launch a radio station. They raised capital by selling stock to their parents and on-air advertising to the local pizza and beauty shops. They cleaned out a closet that was the old ticket booth, next to the gym, and hot-wired their music player and microphones into the intercom system. I started noticing that the six kids had turned into 20. They asked if they could come to school early and work on the project. This was passionate learning in action.

Ralph Fiore and I went on to co-create the Wings program, and after more than 15 years, it still helps high school kids run real businesses, including a radio/TV station, newspaper, bistro, school store, and cafe. We underestimated the demand for this experience as participation has grown to over one-third the school population. The business ideas, both successes and failures, came from the

Students from eVenture 2009

students. The teacher acts as a facilitator, creating an environment that nurtures the "just-in-time learning" model. As students uncover a need, the teacher locates experts (typically local entrepreneurs) and resources. However, the kids are responsible for everything that happens in the business, including their own learning.

The Cooperative Entrepreneurship philosophy, when shared with the next generation, creates exciting results. Imagine the outcome if we could expose every student to Cooperative Entrepreneurship.

Growing Ideas

Cooperative Entrepreneurship requires that you create an environment that encourages innovative thinking, and Charter Partners has taken that requirement to the nth degree. Located in Williams Township, Pennsylvania, Charter Farms is our place where "ideas grow." Situated on 47 acres of pastoral land with a forest backdrop, Charter Farms provides a perfect creative setting for our group meetings and events. Here members can escape from the glass and steel of their offices and co-create solutions for their businesses.

We offer a number of locations for idea generation, like the 270-year-old farmhouse, a converted barn, and a cabin in the woods. No real farm would be complete without animals. When you visit Charter Farms, you'll have the pleasure of meeting our llamas Fanny, Tippy, Milton, and Rudy.

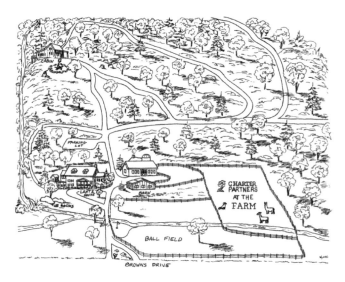

The CE Eco-System

Something very interesting happens when you put these ideas together. I saw it for the first time as I prepared for a meeting in November 2008.

1. Charter Partners Alliance-successful companies using CE to be more successful.

2. Charter Partners Institute-New entrepreneurs using CE to become successful.

3. Charter Farms-Place to practice Cooperative Entrepreneurship.

Combining these ideas created an ecosystem, similar to ones you see in the environment, but one that supports people in an economy. James Moore first used this term to describe economic communities in 1993, describing it as organisms of the business world. One of the best examples I can think of is the Apple iPhone business ecosystem. Think about the vast community of people that now depend on the iPhone to sustain themselves through design, assembly, programming, sales distribution, technical support, third-party developers, artists, investors, and customers.

When I thought about our business ecosystem, I saw a network of young entrepreneurs working together with senior entrepreneurs, creating a regenerative system where all parties could win. The mature organizations received an influx of ideas, energy, and new investment opportunities, while the newer organizations received experience, connections, and capital they needed to survive. The system will get stronger and more diverse over time. The question we faced was how do you connect all the pieces?

I met Jeff Vacha in the 80s when I ran a pre-Internet bulletin board system (BBS) and over the years, we've built a number of experimental online communities. I asked Jeff to help me co-create a community where members can experience CE, where an army of trusted entrepreneurs could mentor aspiring entrepreneurs. In the process, we could build a business ecosystem of creativity and innovation. Jeff, Glen and I partnered to co-create bizeco.com.

Entrepreneurs can come here if they already have an idea in development or they can get invited to join another member's idea. Either way, we're building a trusted community of entrepreneurs helping entrepreneurs. We're excited by the community's potential to change the lonely, arduous experience of a traditional entrepreneur into a collaborative laboratory of people and resources.

Below is a graphical example of the Charter Partners ecosystem.

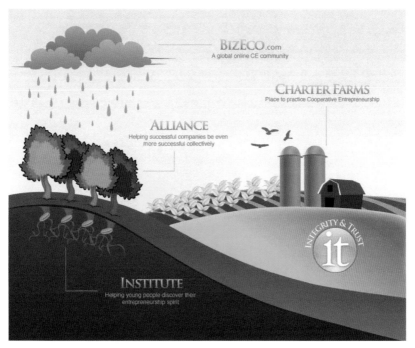

Lessons Learned:

1. You can use symbols that are fun to convey a serious message.

2. Dad was right about trust.

3. It's easy to think trust is a soft concept; in reality it has a hard impact on your bottom line.

4. Everyone on the team is important and can be entrepreneurial.

5. Leading a new initiative requires champions.

6. Only partner with those that share your values.

7. When things are going wrong, communication is even more important.

8. A great partnership is when both parties feel they got the better end of the deal.

9. Small and mid-sized business can collaborate to accomplish things they didn't once imagine.

10. Having a faciligrator can speed the process of innovation.

11. Many students are entrepreneurial and will take responsibility for their own learning.

12. Having a physical and online location will help foster CE.

13. The CE ecosystem connects experienced entrepreneurs to the next generation.

We Need it 3

Born in 1962, I've since learned that the world is an amazing place. I must admit, it can be intimidating. I received no instructions about where I'm going or what I'm supposed to do once I get there. Yet, people like me and you have accomplished some pretty amazing things.

We've harnessed electricity, learned to fly, moved on and under water, and even reached space. Along the way, we uncovered the mysteries of atomic particles and micro-organisms, developed communication tools that fit in the palm of our hands, and created complex economic systems that allow us to access and use vast resources.

However, our achievements have come at a price. We have abused the earth, creating a potential ecological nightmare. One-third of us (2 billion people) still live in poverty. In the last 100 years alone, we have killed over 100 million of each other, on purpose, over control of territory and ideology. No less than three quarters of the countries in our world are perceived to be corrupt.

Take a look at this map from Transparency International[4]. They call it a Corruption Perception Index. The darker colors represent countries with the worst corruption and lighter colors show countries with less corruption. You can see the problem that we're facing in the world.

Question:

Where are we now?

It would be foolish to talk about where we need to go if we did not have an understanding of how we got here. For this reason, it is important we take a little time to do a broad overview of our socioeconomic past. This chapter has been fortified by my collaborator Robert Porter Lynch who has an extensive background in business history and economics.

Capitalism

Our 300-year-old experiment with capitalism has created more wealth and brought more people out of poverty than any other system in human history. However, it is far from perfect and not yet complete. Capitalism, despite its success, requires an upgrade.

The basis of modern capitalism is rooted in Adam Smith's classic book, *Wealth of Nations*, which advocates money and self-interest as the basis of economic power. He wrote his treatise in 1776, during a pre-industrial age, when commerce was highly localized.

Soon thereafter, the early 1800s brought the Industrial Age. Wealthy individuals constructed vast empires in textiles, steel, chemicals, and railroads. Labor, then seen as a commodity, could be used to run machines. Sweatshops emerged, business exploited labor, especially children, and the environment became polluted. Robber-baron capitalism concentrated enormous wealth in the hands of a few, making the rich richer and the poor poorer.

An uncontrolled roller coaster of prosperity and depression ruled the economies of Europe and North America for over a century. Boom times were followed by depressions as the banking system cycled from greed-driven profit making, then economies recoiled as the bubbles burst. Imperialistic nations spread capitalism across the globe in search of undeveloped nations with exploitable natural resources.

To understand the 2008 financial meltdown, one must understand history and the factors that caused similar past debacles. This type of economic crash has occurred every 20-30 years (or more), sometimes with catastrophic effects. In Europe and the United States, previous crashes happened in 1636, 1694, 1721, 1792, 1797, 1819, 1825, 1847, 1857, 1873, 1890, 1893, 1907, 1929, and now 2008. Japan had a total meltdown of its financial system in the 1990s, and we experienced smaller regional or industry specific crashes in the U.S. during the 1980s in real estate, silver, and Internet stocks.

Leading up to the 2008 meltdown, we witnessed the return of Robber Baron Capitalism. Banks, driven by the drumbeat of their Wall Street brethren for ever-increasing profits, learned from their credit card experience to entice people into a bigger game—buy a house on credit through sub-prime lending. They then hit the low-income, sub-prime homeowners with an Adjustable Rate Mortgage that would produce higher returns several years later. Also adding fuel was government intervention in the form of pressure to provide mortgages to the unqualified borrower. This hurricane made landfall with explosive force, causing some to believe capitalism was the problem.

Communism and Socialism

Communism developed as a reaction to the exploitive capitalists and the robber barons who would win at all costs, even peoples' lives. Karl Marx wrote the Communist Manifesto in 1848 to counteract the capitalist extremists. He envisioned a classless society that would be the ultimate evolution to human development. Marx proposed a communistic system that returned all the wealth and control to the working class, framing this as the struggle between labor and capital. Marx proposed that labor, not capital, was the rightful foundation of economic wealth and to protect people from the robber barons, a new social and economic order was necessary. By 1848, Europe was awash in riots and revolutions as the workers revolted against capitalists, giving birth to the labor union movement. Russia, in 1918, and later China, adopted Marx's system.

What they didn't realize was that communism inspires little creativity and leaves little room for individual passion. A homogenized communistic or socialistic system is boring at best. A lack of passion creates a whole new kind of energy shortage in an economy.

Although less extreme and more balanced, socialism still suffers the same fate as communism. Apathy and atrophy are more common as society waits to be taken care of. The government becomes the caretaker, and, due to its size and the speed of bureaucracy, the innovations that need to happen to keep up with change come too slowly

By the way, the same robber barons types found in capitalism found their way to the top and exploited these systems too.

Question:

What is the upgrade capitalism needs?

Capitalism is essentially an alliance of five powerful interests: business (providing goods and services), labor (producing goods and services), investors (providing financial capital to grow businesses), consumers (to buy goods and services), and government (setting up and enforcing the rules). When this alliance works efficiently, capitalism is a highly productive system, the best the world has known.

What makes a great game? Let's put these relationships in modern terms. Picture yourself at a sporting event. Think about how the same basic principles of balance apply to a great game. The stadium represents a capitalist system;

1. Owners (Investors) want to make a return on their investment, but understand and love the game as well.

2. Coaches (CEO's) prepare the players for competition.

3. Players (Employees) are passionate and want to win.

4. Referees (Government) call a fair game.

5. Fans (Customers) fill the stadium, passionately rooting for their team.

When the game is over, there's a winner and a loser. Each team then shakes hands, debriefs what they learned, and goes home, hopefully to play another day. Everybody leaves feeling they got their money's worth, win or lose.

Now envision the "nightmare" game, perhaps a dirty hit that seriously injures a player, overzealous fans fighting in the stands, coaches controlling their players every move, or referees who have already decided which team should win and owners exacerbating the problem by demanding short term results. I have been at games like this, and when the integrity of the game is compromised, everyone loses. Fans leave disappointed, player's sports careers are ended, coaches feel robbed, and the referees run for their lives and owners lose their investment.

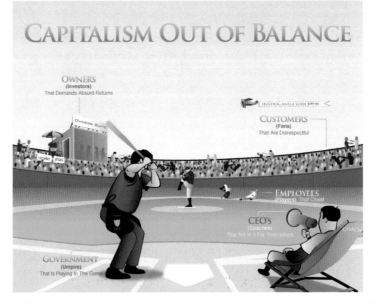

When business is conducted in a corrupt culture, companies cheat, rob, or steal their way to the top. Once cheating or unfair advantage is introduced, the competitors are encouraged to show less integrity, setting off a domino effect of deeper corruption. Talk soon turns to law making where socialistic controls attempt to level the playing field, effectively putting government "in the game" as opposed to maintaining controls. That is capitalism out of balance.

When played by the rules, capitalism works. It's energizing. It brings out one's best skills and provides personal rewards. Competition can be fun. Coke vs. Pepsi; Apple vs. Microsoft; Google vs. Yahoo; or Cowboys vs. Eagles. If the game is invigorating, innovative, playful, and energizing, people will want to be part of the experience. By nature, we want to be on a winning team. Healthy competition is good for all of us, and when in balance, we all benefit.

Question:

What's next for capitalism?

We're at the birth of the Innovation Age. Over the last 300 years, we moved from conquering and exploiting nature to trying to save it; from controlling labor to empowering people; and from command and control management to trusted networks. In the Innovation Age, new integrations between computers and

HISTORY OF HUMAN COMMERCE

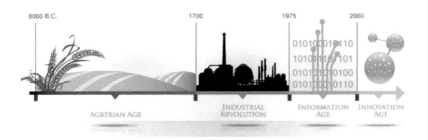

telecommunications have enabled networking in ways never imagined just a few years ago. Business arch rivals are now collaborating. Intellectual power and trusted networks are supplanting capital, the previous source of power in business.

Social responsibility is considered an integral part of a business's mandate. Many businesses are aligning their strategic direction using alliance-based business networks. The power of alliance networks will depend on their ability to innovate rapidly. This is the new Innovation Age of capitalism.

Question:

What are the new economics of the Innovation Age?

Expandables

An expandable is different from an expendable. When you use a gallon of gasoline, the gasoline is gone forever. Each gallon of gas you use diminishes the supply of gas. As demand goes up, supply goes down, driving the price up. That is an expendable.

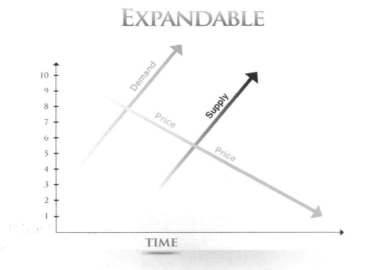

EXPANDABLE

Expandables are not limited by supply and demand in fact the more they are used the less the cost, just the opposite of what we learned in Economics 101. The more expandables are used the more valuable they become. They don't wear out like a tire or a machine. Think about Facebook[5], Twitter[6], and Google[7]. They are all examples of expandables. The more you use them the more valuable they become, but strangely they cost you virtually nothing

The Internet itself is also an expandable as are eBay, Wikipedia, Amazon, Lynx, and Kiva. They all use a community to keep innovating and incorporate a peer-based feedback system to keep the community honest.

The Innovation Age can be confusing, and people can easily get caught between the shifts. If you're not on the expandable train it can be a frustrating experience. The rapidity of the shifts between the Industrial, Information, and Innovation Ages over the last thirty years caught many by surprise. What was considered truth in one era becomes a myth in the next. Worse, educators are teaching old management principles that were true just a few years ago. Of course, where there is great change, there is also great opportunity.

Speed

Darwin is often quoted as saying the world is based on survival of the fittest. What he actually said was, "It is not the strongest of the species that survives, nor the most intelligent, but the one most responsive to change." To say it more directly, "Adapt or die!"

If our success is tied to our ability to adapt, then we need to become more like the Internet. Our world is shifting at a rate

---

[5] Facebook is a global social networking website. Users can add friends and send them messages, and update their personal profiles. (www.facebook.com)

[6] Twitter, a microblogging service, allows users to tweet in 140 characters about what they're doing. (www.twitter.com)

[7] An Internet search engine that provides e-mail, online mapping, office productivity, social networking, and video sharing services. (www.google.com)

never before seen. Consider the results of a survey done over the last five years.[8]

Senior executives (45-65 years of age from every size and type of business) were asked to plot a curve given a simple set of instructions: "What does the rate of change feel like?" Astoundingly, 80-90% responded with a curve that looked like the Acceleration of Change chart.[9]

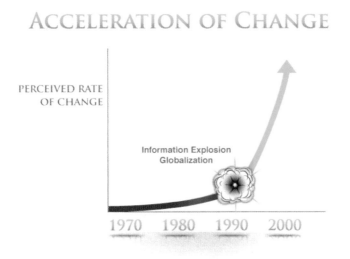

ACCELERATION OF CHANGE

We're in a period where change is happening at an increasing rate, challenging our ability to keep pace. Every entrepreneur must now consider how these issues impact his or her business.

---

[8] During the last 5 years, Robert Porter Lynch, in speeches, seminars, and workshops, asked over 10,000 executives across the US and Canada about how change, speed, and complexity has changed. Between 80-90% of all audiences responded with the curve noted.

[9] The only difference among these 90% was the point of inflection where the curve changes direction radically. For those in very rapid change industries, such as high tech, the point was generally between 1986 and 1990. For those in slower changing businesses, such as petro-chemicals the point tended toward 1995-7. The primary reasons for the shift cited by executives were: computers, faxes, globalization, cell phones, then the internet, each compounding upon the other.

Transparency

Lately, I've attended gatherings with some of the world's leading social media people. Critics say these individuals are a bunch of self-absorbed tech geeks tweeting about their lives. I found these gatherings very different. Something else happens there, and it has nothing to do with technology. A powerful undercurrent of honesty and openness drives this community of people. Here they talk about giving more than they get. I see it changing the way we view the world.

For example, at Gnomedex I was playing with a new tabletop computer, Microsoft Surface, when someone put down a book called *Trust Agents*. I've been writing this book for a long time and found very little published material on the subject of trust. I immediately wanted to know who wrote it. I soon found out it was Chris Brogan, an author and top blogger. He was at the conference, and we talked for a few minutes. I mentioned to Chris that I was almost finished with my book on trust in business and was looking for an editor. You might think another author would be protective of his resources with the competition, instead he recommended Britt Raybould, who it turns out was very helpful to me in refining the book. When I wrote to him to thank him for recommending her, he said no thanks needed, just tell more people about her, which I am doing now. That's the "pay it forward" culture that I see changing the way we do business.

I found that same attitude of giving and sharing throughout the Gnomedex conference. These folks are all about creating new ways of sharing and connecting, at lightning speed. They are setting the pace for global change. The world they are creating is transparent, honest, and giving.

That's the good news and the bad news. Now what happens in your business, or your life, can be and probably will be, broadcast so that anyone can learn about it. If your company is doing things honestly, people will rave about you, and your business will grow. If your company is dishonest, with poor customer service, you'll be on Facebook and tweeted about before your customer service rep hangs up the phone.

In the fable "The Emperors New Clothes" two weavers convince the emperor they have the ablity to create a suit that is invisable to people who are unfit or incompetant at their job. The emporer proudly wears his new suit getting compliments from all his subjects, until one day, a child yells out, "he is wearing nothing at all!"

The new economy is like that child, it wants honesty and integrity and will "call out" something that does not look right.

What does transparency in business look like? Gary Vaynerchuk, a leading wine expert, can sell an entire stock of wine with a single tweet. How? Because he's established a trusted relationship with a vast network of people. He believes everyone has a chance to have the influence of Oprah. If he's right, and I believe he is, you must protect the integrity of your personal and corporate brand with your life, because it says everything about you. In this new world, your ability to influence is directly related to your ability to create

> The only way to succeed today is to be completely transparent.
>
> - Gary Vaynerchuk

trusted networks. The new rules mean you're never really off the field. You can't be an SOB at work and a Boy Scout leader at home.

The Information and Innovation Ages have brought us closer together. The world is smaller, and it's easier to look into each other's windows, both real and virtual. This transparency provides us with a new view of our lives and our businesses. With our every move digitally recorded and broadcasted around the world in real time, we no longer have a place to hide. Separation no longer exists, making integrity the new gold standard. It's a new kind of transparency where your grandchildren are going to know you by the digital DNA you are leaving behind on the Internet. What do you want your legacy to be?

Lessons Learned

1. Corruption is killing us, literally.
2. Capitalism needs an upgrade.
3. The government needs to referee the game, they should not be playing on the field.
4. We are in a new Age of Innovation.
5. New behaviors are needed.
6. Cooperative Entrepreneurship is an expandable.
7. The rate of change is increasing at an increasing rate.
8. The world is transparent.
9. If you go to a game don't start a fight with the other team, you will probably be on youtube by the time you get home.

Examples of it 4

We've just discussed capitalism's evolution and how it's provided an amazing environment for the great innovations of our time that improved the quality of life for millions. By far the best of the systems, however, capitalism has left us with a morality hangover. We have all suffered from the acts of individuals who think capitalism is a license for greed, control, and disrespect for people and the environment. If we continue down this path, corruption will become so prevalent that the future could be much worse than the past. As I mentioned before, capitalism needs an upgrade, but how and to what?

I have an answer! It's likely not the only answer, or even the whole answer, but it is an answer. We know it works on a small scale, and I believe it can work on a large scale. The answer comes from bringing together our story and the world's story—Cooperative Entrepreneurship.

Question:

What can CE change in our lives?

To help you understand how I made the leap from a public school insurance alliance, to an upgrade for capitalism, I invite you to see the world as I see it. Imagine a young women who is about to become a Cooperative Entrepreneur, we'll call her Emily. She lives in a world where the CE culture is woven into every aspect of the community (education, business and government, etc.). Now let's explore her life in four situations: 1) her education, 2) starting her business, 3) sustaining her business, and 4) the prosperity of her community.

CE in Education

In a school that embraces CE Emily learns about the real need for creative thinking. Access to the Internet has changed forever what and how we need to learn, and she's been well trained in research methods, letting the computer handle routine analytical functions. In addition to learning how to read, write, and solve math and science problems, part of her school day includes uncovering a new problem and creating a solution for it.

> Galen Godbey of DeSales University, shared with me recent results from a study conducted by The Conference Board. The study asked K12 superintendents to identify the most important skill that students needed to learn. Their collective answer was "problem solving." When business leaders were asked the same question, their collective answer was "problem identification." This subtle difference, makes all the difference and is at the very heart of our work at the Institute.

Emily uses her life experience, to find things that need improving. Her solution starts by persuading her classmates to team up (learning to form a team) and collaborate. Her teachers faciligrate by connecting the team to key resources, inside and outside the school, as Emily brings her idea to reality. Whatever career she chooses—accountant, musician, artist, doctor, welder, fashion designer, philosopher—her success will depend on her ability to find needs and fulfill them.

At Charter Partners Institute our student experiences have shown that even the best educated students, when challenged to think about the world like a series of problems to solve, struggle to create ideas. Recently, during one of our summer programs, an especially bright young man told me it took him almost 48 hours to understand this method of problem solving. In the beginning, he was so frustrated, having never been asked to practice this type of thinking. After two days, a thought came to him for an iPhone application, and then the ideas started to flow. He and his teammates stayed up late at night talking about all the possibilities.

Imagine if we were to engage the minds of all our youth in creative idea generation, innovations would come at a pace unseen previously. Incidentally, one of the Institute mentors was amazed that it only took two days for this idea to form. Think about it…after only two days, he came up with a viable business idea. Even in our fast-paced world that's astounding!

What would your life be like now if the environment in your school had encouraged this type of creative thinking? The longer we wait to allow our youth to exercise their creativity the harder it will be to tap into their ideas as they get buried under all the routine knowledge. Cooperative Entrepreneurship needs to become part of the lexicon of learning now.

A CE Start Up

Emily has graduated from school and wants to start her own business. Luckily, she's been practicing for this moment. She knows that in a traditional business environment (non-CE), three out of five businesses fail in the first five years.

But that is not how Emily will choose to start her business. As a Cooperative Entrepreneur, she knows the rules have changed. While not easy, it is better. Over the years, Emily has been exposed to many mentors and nurtured a network of trusted advisors, building her team along the way. With her innovative idea, she goes to her team to find support and advice. This team has developed a high level of internal trust so she can share her idea with less fear.

On the team may be a venture capitalist who helps make the idea stronger and worthy of new investment dollars. Perhaps another team member has started a business and will share that experience so she can grow. With Cooperative Entrepreneurship, Emily is no longer one person struggling to find resources. Instead, she's a community of people who have come together to strengthen an idea and ensure a business survives.

What about ownership? Does that change? There are many potential ownership models. Some members of the team may be there to give and receive knowledge with no other expectations. Others may participate through a consulting model, and some may help to advance an idea through an ownership interest. Cooperative Entrepreneurship is live and dynamic and I anticipate new models will be developed as more businesses embrace resource sharing. I also believe using this method will change the 60% failure rate after five years to an 80% success rate for new businesses.

CE Sustaining Business

At this stage, Emily's business has matured into a growing concern. Cooperative Entrepreneurship is now part of her DNA. Born and raised in it, she naturally make it part of her business culture. She teaches it to her employees, and they in turn teach it to the vendors and customers, keeping a steady stream of innovation coming their way. This philosophy keeps Emily in business and she uses it to collaborate with others by joining, or creating, a Cooperative Entrepreneurship Alliance (CEA). Here is how she'll go about putting one together.

1. CEA starts with a Champion (Gino).

2. The Champion invites a few respected peers to join a team (Presidents' Day).

3. Peers invite a larger group, eventually building a small team (12).

4. The team organizes around a common opportunity (WHIP).

5. An opportunity arises, requiring some risk taking (Repotting).

6. Risk can only be taken with people whom you trust (Trust Towel).

7. Trust builds and allows for innovations (owned insurance company).

8. Innovations are done best with peers (Al Van Riper).

9. CEAs sometimes need organizational help (Faciligrator).

10. A successful CEA finds ways to nurture the next generation of entrepreneurs (Wings).

To give the group some structure, once the CEA is formed the members typically sign a code of conduct document. Charter Partners calls it a Declaration of Interdependence.

Once a trusted relationship bond exists, Emily's group will start to look at coopertunities. Here are the Top 10 Coopertunities that come out of many groups.

1. Shared Marketing

2. Common Procurement

3. Shared Investment Opportunities

4. Shared Human Resource/Recruitment

5. Common Information Technology

6. Shared Financial Management

7. Shared Board of Advisors

8. Shared Meeting Facility

9. Succession Planning

10. Foundation supporting Young Entrepreneurs

The CEAs are designed to benefit the entire network, especially the consumer. They get the benefits of reduced costs, and innovative products and services. Membership in a CEA is never forced or controlled by any one organization. Membership ebbs and flows, with CEAs formed voluntarily based on needs. They also disassemble if it is appropriate. They are never used to reduce competition, price fix, or as a leverage weapon. Any action in this vein is illegal and the polar opposite of Cooperative Entrepreneurship values.

A fractal is best described as a reduced-size copy of the whole. A fern is an example. Look at the plant, then the branch ,and then the leaf. The branch and leaves are simply reduced copies of the whole. It has a pattern that is repeated over and over again creating the overall plant.

Emily's CEA is, in fact, part of something even larger. She has learned to think of it as a fractal. CEA groups have a common mission, values, and communication methods. In essence, they duplicate themselves many times over, creating exponential value. Using a shared culture, shared mission, and shared resources, a group of groups can innovate at an amazing rate. Think about the bottom line issues of new sales opportunities, the chance to consolidate costs, and the raw economics.

This model can work for almost any size business; it can be individuals working together or very large organizations. The typical size business forming CEAs with the Charter Partners organization has sales of about $8,000,000. Using round numbers a CEA with 12 members would have **$100,000,000** in revenue and if you established 12 CEA's in an area it would represent a **$1 billion in revenue.**

With that kind of economic power, just think about the new resources Emily would have. Now think about her ability to innovate with all that intellectual power, especially if each company included all of their employees on the team (remember my lawn maintenance guy).

In January 2005, Charter Partners wanted to demonstrate how this works. We brought seven of our CEA leaders together for the purpose of creating an alliance between the alliances. At this meeting, a Declaration of Interdependence was drafted and signed by these members. This declaration created a larger network that enabled Charter Partners to create a larger community.

Charter Partners signing of the - Declaration of Interdependence.
L to R Dave Dillon, Tom Kardish, Jim Germak, Gabe Vitale, Al Van Riper, John Lawlor, Bob Wilson.

Prosperity of a Community

Emily lives in an area known as Lehigh Valley, Pennsylvania, a great place to live and work. Located one hour from Philadelphia and New York, things have changed since Billy Joel wrote his sad song about Allentown. The demise of Bethlehem Steel opened up the canopy of the forest and allowed for re-growth. Within the Valley's borders are 14 institutions of higher education, one of the largest Chambers of Commerce in the county with 5,000 members, two world-class hospital systems, and amazing companies like Crayola, Martin Guitar, Olympus, and Air Products. The Valley is at the intersection of two major highways and has sprawling industrial parks. For pleasure, there is an expansive arts community, two rivers, and great hiking, biking, and skiing nearby. All this activity is capped off with 300 years of living Moravian history.

Emily knows Lehigh Valley could be more.

Most students that come to the universities leave to work in other communities and most of the venture capital from the area goes to fund companies outside the region. The hospitals are more rivals than collaborators. The economic development people are underfunded and overworked, as they try to attract a few good companies to the region. As great as the individual companies are, there is a need for ongoing economic development to keep the community healthy.

As a successful Cooperative Entrepreneur, Emily imagines applying her resources to help the community, starting the way most other entrepreneurs start, with a vision. It might go something like this, "The Lehigh Valley is going to be the number one Innovation Center of America. A place where we can be a leading source of successful start-up companies, more than any other community."

Imagine a community on that kind of mission. What kind of energy could it unleash? What kind of people could be attracted to the area? What cooperation would need to happen to make it a reality? The great thing about a vision? It brings people together to see something greater than themselves. With this kind of mission, many more might be willing to take some risks and lend a hand as they see the long-term benefit for themselves as well as the community. Now you've got the idea, but how do you make things happen?

Emily might start, by looking at what other cities like Boston, Philadelphia, and Tampa are doing. At the state level, Michigan's governor, Jennifer Granholm, took a serious interest in revitalizing an economy devastated by the loss of auto manufacturing. With their CoolCities.com initiative, the state and the governor understand that they can't mandate, structure, or take over creativity. Doing so would be akin to the government (referees) becoming the players on the field. It's about creating and supporting a collaborative environment.

She may also suggest that others on the team read Richard Florida's book, *The Rise of the Creative Class*. He addresses a common myth about economic development. Some communities believed that attracting big companies would sustain new job development. Many tried to turn themselves into the next "Silicon Somewhere" by building high-tech office and industrial parks supplemented by venture capital funds.

Florida found that these lured companies eventually left the area for other communities with a bigger pool of creative people. In a curious reversal, people weren't moving to jobs as often as companies were moving to creative communities. He uncovered a direct correlation between the diversity of people and economic prosperity. The density of the artists, writers, performers, and the gay population has an impact on the community's success. Restaurants and shops follow the artists, attracting talented people who want to live in a vibrant, diverse culture that stimulates their senses. Companies looking for talent move their headquarters to this environment (e.g., fishermen go to the fish) and it builds on itself, creating an innovative ecosystem. As the creative community strengthens, so does the economy and business. What could your community accomplish if it embraced Cooperative Entrepreneurship?

Hopefully the examples of how CE applies to Emily's life gives you a few ideas about how you can apply it to yours. This new way of thinking is exciting but it comes at the risk of people mistaking CE for being a softer or weaker version of capitalism. CE is a better way to compete, it brings out the best of human nature and focuses it on creating solutions. In todays fast paced transparent world, innovation and integrity are competitive advantages in themselves. There is nothing weak about doing things right, it's just the opposite it makes you strong. The next chapter gives you insights into the three key principles of CE.

Lessons Learned

1. CE can be applied throughout the entrepreneurial life cycle.

2. CE can be applied to help education keep up with our changing world.

3. CE can be applied to the start-up phase of a company, improving the chances of survival.

4. CE can be applied to an existing business to help sustain and grow it.

5. CE can be applied to foster economic development in a community.

6. Doing the right thing with the right people is a competitive advantage.

Principles of  5

When I was growing up, my family lived by certain principles. I did not have to think about what was right or wrong. We knew what was expected. These principles were invisible, but guided my every decision.

The guiding principles of Cooperative Entrepreneurship are easy to remember: **Think**, **Team**, and **Trust**. These three principles are key to the success of every Cooperative Entrepreneur. If you remove even one, the system may work, but it's not Cooperative Entrepreneurship. The synergy between Think, Team, and Trust make work. Let's examine each principle.

Principle #1: Think

You are the owner of a creative, mysterious, and powerful device. This device gives you the ability to bring to life whatever you can dream up. It has unlimited capacity to imagine and learn. It can record every second of your life and play it back. It can tell stories, create music, art, and movies. It has such fine motor control it allows you to perform brain surgery and gymnastics. It can calculate so precisely we can land a man on the moon and split an atom. The more you use it, the more valuable it becomes, it's an expandable. Its potential is so vast it is impossible for us to grasp. That's the good news.

Now the bad news . . . this device arrived without a manual and is subject to being easily distracted. Worse, not everyone is using their creative device for positive purposes. Sadly, many people stop using their device altogether. For example, look at what happens to our creativity as we age:

CREATIVITY AT GENIUS LEVEL

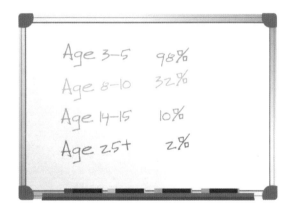

Age 3-5   98%

Age 8-10   32%

Age 14-15 10%

Age 25+   2%

Practicing the Think Principle exercises your brain so that it stays young and flexible. My friend, Jason Magdison, wrote a book called *Idealized Design* that describes how much space there actually is to grow our minds.

Jason's breakdown of User Research/Design puts this space into perspective. The green slice represents, "What you know" about people's needs and desires. The blue slice represents the efforts we make to learn, "What you know you don't know." These are things that we, but not necessarily customers, for example, feel are important. The purple slice, "What you don't know you don't know," only comes into play if we get customers to open up about what is most important to them. When you're asked to design "What hasn't yet been created," you've entered the red slice. Here you ask people to start fresh, creating an ideal design, and the addition of your skill set brings the innovation to life. Thinking in this way opens up entirely new avenues of opportunity.

IDEALIZED DESIGN KNOWLEDGE CHART

Question:

Where does creativity start?

Entrepreneurs lead by developing a passionate vision of the future. Where do they get it? The vision comes from doing something they love. This love gives them insight into a product or service and provides the courage and tenacity to overcome the inevitable obstacles.

What does turning your love into world-class business opportunity look like? Each of the following people had a passion for an idea and made it come to life. I hope you can take inspiration from their passion.

Seth Goldman, one of my favorite entrepreneurial success stories makes a perfect example for the Think Principle. I first met Seth when he spoke at the 2004 Gel Conference in New York City.

Fitness is important to Seth, and after a particularly parched run through Central Park in 1997, he wanted a drink that was more than just water,

> **Your work is going to fill a large part of your life, and the only way to be truly satisfied is to do what you believe is great work; and the only way to do great work is to love what you do.**
> Steve Jobs

but not full of sugar. Failing to find one, Seth decided to reignite an old conversation on the love for tea with his Yale professor, Barry Nalebuff. While traveling through the tea-drinking cultures of India, China, and Russia, both developed a love for good tea.

Seth and Barry decided the marketplace needed a low-sugar, high-quality organic tea. Barry suggested the name Honest Tea, and it immediately resonated with Seth. Taking a risk, Seth left his marketing and sales post with a socially responsible mutual fund and launched Honest Tea from his home's guest room. After brewing the tea in his kitchen, he put five large thermoses in his car and drove to the local Whole Foods regional office. Based on five thermoses, he convinced the general purchasing manager to order 15,000 bottles. Honest Tea had its first customer and quickly became the best-selling organic tea throughout the Whole Foods chain. Coke eventually purchased a 40% interest in

Honest Tea, now the number one organic tea drink in America.

Mel Zuckerman told me his personal story when I visited him in Tucson, Arizona. He turned one of the worst experiences of his life into a passion to help others. In the process, he re-invented an industry.

Mel was with his father the day the doctors told his dad he would die of lung cancer. He saw his father rip

> Why Climb Mount Everest? - George Mallory was the first to try. He said, "What I get from this adventure is sheer joy." Mallory died in June 1924 doing what he loved. His body was found yards away from the summit. No one knows if he ever made it to the top. It was an awesome failure!

his cigarettes from his pocket and crush them, saying he would quit, but it was too late. Mel lost his father, and the experience affected him deeply. He took a break from his real estate company and invested in his own health.

After four weeks spent at a "fat farm," he called his wife. "I know what I want to do with the rest of my life," he said. They liquidated their real estate holdings and purchased a former dude ranch in Tucson to start America's first destination health resort, Canyon Ranch. Mel didn't experience immediate success, but he learned and adapted until it worked financially. By taking the risk to pursue what he loved, he created a place that has healed untold numbers of people. You can now find the industry-leading Canyon Ranch in Arizona, Massachusetts, Florida, Nevada and aboard numerous cruise ships.

Tony Salvaggio founder of Computer Aid in Allentown, Pennsylvania, created one of the world's most respected information technology companies. With over $250,000,000 in sales, Computer Aid employs 2,500 professionals all over the world. Tony was an IBM'er for 20 years when he made the difficult choice to strike out on his own. He loves his family and he loves the Lehigh Valley and to continue his success at IBM would mean moving multiple times over many years and never really being an entrepreneur, which was Tony's dream. Tony decided to start his business from scratch, by himself. My conversations with Tony could fill another book but, at the core, he credits his mother and father for his success. His mother taught him the love of reading, which he says has been the most important professional asset he ever developed.

Tony says that success as an entrepreneur requires you know your business area or space extremely well. Well enough to be able to lead and craft new innovations that offer customer value well beyond what the current state provides. To know a space, he suggests making it a habit to constantly read and in-take as much information and knowledge as you can in both your immediate professional or business area, as well as general business management and eclectic topics that stimulate your mind. Tony, for example, had been an avid science fiction reader for many years and his shelves hold dozens of books on a variety of topics.

When it comes to living one's life over a period of decades, Tony remembers his father saying, "Whatever you do, son, don't drift. You are better off changing direction 10 times in pursuit of what you love, but don't drift." Tony believes that everyone, no matter how old, should always think about improving themselves and even recreating themselves. Tony, graduated as an engineer and progressed to general management over a decades long period. He encourages everyone to pursue what they love. He cites as an example a key, long-term employee who left his company to be a teacher. She is pursuing what she loves, and he is thrilled for her!

He advises that you should look forward and imagine a personal future state that encompasses your ambition, as well as personal non-business goals. His advice is to think and imagine who you want to become and then begin to walk down that road, day by day. Think about the person you ideally would like to evolve into as a person.

Importantly, write all this down, and continually reread it. Tony says he is still trying hard to picture his future state, even though many people his age are retired. In Tony's world life is indeed both an adventure and a challenge to use your skills as best as possible, while having a lot of fun along the way.

Jared Isaacman from United Bank Card in Clinton, New Jersey, took a passion and turned it into a world-class business, too. At 16, he left high school to work for a company that processed credit cards. He loved technology and learned the credit card processing business from the ground up. He often asked, "Why do we do it this way?" They, of course, answered, "Because we've always done it this way."

Dissatisfied, Jared kept asking questions until he knew enough about the system to realize it was layered with inefficiency. He knew it could be done better. At home, Jared set up shop with some friends and designed a system to simplify the process, reducing the number of steps and people involved. He dug into every aspect of the business until he reduced the inefficiency, saving money for thousands of businesses.

Jared destroyed the old model of processing credit cards, turned the industry on its head, and made millions for himself and his family in the process. Today, his company processes billions of dollars in transactions each year. His is one of America's fastest growing companies. Outside of business, Jared travels around the world, setting new speed records for private jet flight, and raising money for the Make a Wish Foundation. By the way, Jared's still in his 20s.

Seth, Mel, Tony, Jared, and other entrepreneurs make new space for all of us. They do what they love and pursue their passions. These four used their insight to achieve success. Seth combined his knowledge of athletes with his love of tea. Mel combined his passion for a personal health transformation with knowledge of construction. Tony combined his love of reading with the pursuit of niche expertise. Jared combined his credit card industry education with a love for technology that provided a new answer. These guys interrupted the status quo, changing the game and creating new ventures.

Through our own experience as a family business, and along with the Charter Partners Institute, we developed the following diagram to express the entrepreneur's innovation model. Think about it. What do you love? What are you experiencing and observing that can be improved? What unique insight do you have? Put your creativity to work. Show us the way to the future. We're about to give you a way to put booster rockets on that idea to help it come to fruition, we call it the Team Principle.

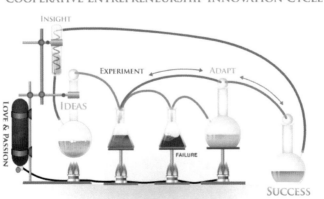

Innovation Cycle concepts developed with Mark Lang, Charter Partners Institute.

Principle #2: Team

The Team Principle is key to the pursuit of Cooperative Entrepreneurship. It takes the benefits of the Think Principle and moves it forward a quantum leap. The advantages of a team versus a lone entrepreneur working on the next big thing should be obvious. Imagine what could happen if we connected the garages and created a network of creative people. People doing what they love, constantly working on ways to improve their world and sharing resources and experience. This is the new team of the Innovation Age.

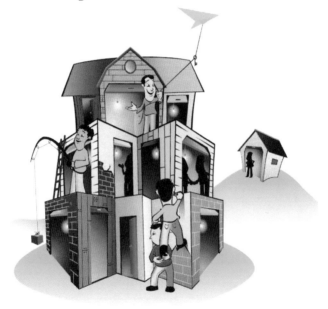

Our future lies not with one genius in a garage, but in connecting the garages together.

Todd Welch

We've discussed how to think like an entrepreneur. Now, as a team, we have the opportunity to build on that foundation, creating a community that can produce many times the innovations of a single entrepreneur. The Team Principle creates a community where everyone gets to be an innovative entrepreneur.

The world's most prolific entertainment company practices the Team Principle. Since premiering *Toy Story* in 1995, Pixar Animation Studios has had one hit after another: *A Bug's Life, Toy Story 2, Monsters, Inc., Finding Nemo, The Incredibles, Cars, Ratatouille, WALL·E,* and *UP.* How do they do it? Pixar calls it Collective Creativity. According to a *Harvard Business Review* interview (September 2008) with Pixar co-founder Ed Catmull,

> If you want to go quickly go alone. If you want to go far go together.
>
> African Proverb

Pixar is a community where relationships matter and it must be safe to tell the truth. The rule is to empower people. Humanity loves heroes, but some of the most exceptional unsung heroes in business are the managers who resist taking authority and the limelight, instead building a stage where others can be stars.

According to Catmull, people tend to think of creativity as a mysterious solo act. However, a movie contains tens of thousands of ideas. They're in the form of every sentence; in the performance of each line; in the design of characters, sets, and backgrounds; in the camera locations; in the colors, the lighting, and the pacing. The director and the other creative leaders of a production do not come up with all

> The only thing I do by myself is use the bathroom.
>
> Scott Welch

the ideas. Rather, every single member of the 200- to 250-person production group makes suggestions. Creativity must be present at every level of every artistic and technical part of the organization. The leaders perform the difficult task of sorting through a mass of ideas to find the ones that fit into a coherent whole, supporting the story. It's like an archaeological dig where you may not know what you're looking for or whether you'll even find anything. The process is downright scary.

Contrast this model with the Industrial Age model of teams. As a project is handed down the line, teams are created to distribute the workload. These teams have a limited view of the whole and are not encouraged to innovate or create something new. It's more about workload distribution. They don't have the whole project in perspective. They are focused on their particular segment.

The former Bethlehem Steel plant followed this model (today, there stands a casino on the plant site that, ironically, had construction delays due to a steel supply shortage). The old employees talk about the days at the steel plant when, in the lunchroom, they were prohibited from sitting with people from other divisions. They had created silos and fiefdoms, isolating themselves from one another. Meanwhile overseas, they figured out how to innovate steel manufacturing, doing it faster and cheaper. Falling behind, Bethlehem, one of the largest companies in the world, was left for scrap iron. The Innovation Age is here, and teams holding on to the Industrial or Information Age model must give way to the innovation teams of tomorrow.

Question:

Can you give me another example?

Charter Partners helped five area golf clubs join together for the purpose of reducing costs and increasing profits. They named the alliance Tee 2 Green (T2G), with the goal of creating new opportunities. T2G immediately identified the easy areas to reduce costs, like purchasing chemicals in volume and consolidating food contracts. The real innovations, however, came in the area of growth. The clubs had experienced a decline in membership and golf rounds

> No matter what accomplishments you make, somebody helps you.
> Althea Gibson

booked due to both the economy and course overbuilding. During one of the alliance meetings, a team member asked a key question, "What if we created a master membership?" They discussed the idea and agreed that a member, who joined the master membership, could play multiple courses. They would also get preferred tee times, use of the locker rooms, and access to club services.

Within weeks, brochures were printed and memberships were sold. Shortly thereafter, an article appeared in a national golf magazine, detailing this innovation as an example of how clubs could weather the economic downturn.

We can't leave the issue of teams without saying something about the amazing relationships that we've seen develop. After many conversations with people in both small and mid-sized companies, I've discovered that no matter what they sell or produce, they believe they're in the relationship business.

People do business with people they trust, and teams are willing to do their best work when team members trust each other. A special bond develops between members that many of you have experienced. After watching dozens of creative teams form and innovate, I'm most amazed by their resilience when things go wrong. Whether they invited the wrong people to the team, failed to foresee a problem, or missed a project timeline, these groups had an excuse to quit, but they didn't. These small groups develop a tight bond that keeps them coming back. After witnessing this phenomenon repeatedly over several years, we adopted a phrase we think is an absolute truism about teams:

> **People support what they help create.**

Question:

What happens when the team changes?

Contributed by Frank DeGeorge, former Charter Partners associate.

When I originally approached Charter Partners and its business model of partnering and sharing knowledge between entrepreneurs, I was a bit skeptical, especially when insurance was added to the mix. Business men and women coming face to face as competitors in their chosen industry sharing business practices and best practices, all in the attempt to better their business and insurance environment, was unheard of. The level of trust needed for such an atmosphere to survive and flourish was too great. Once I started at Charter Partners, I realized I was wrong. This model not only worked, but, over the years of my employment, it took off in many different directions, all with the trust in the re-insurer acting as the adhesive keeping it together. The Charter Partners Community was in full swing, and in later years, the Charter Partners Captive flourished.

> Our ambitions must be broad enough to include the aspirations and needs of others, for their sakes and for our own.
>
> Cesar Chavez

The model began to crack when the trust of the re-insurer, the alliance adhesive, was broken. This breach of trust rippled through the community. Charter Partners management was caught off guard. Being on the front lines of underwriting, it wasn't long before business was lost and my employment came to a sad end.

However, I was given full access to the company computers, phones, and faxes for three months while I searched for new employment, a situation unheard of in today's business environment. I still received full pay and benefits, too. Free to come and go as I wished, I felt Charter Partners tried to make the situation as best they could for me under the circumstances. The personal and professional growth over my seven years at Charter Partners was instrumental in securing my present employment. I will always be grateful for that.

The corporate world is full of back stabbing, all in an attempt to climb that corporate ladder, but at what price? From day one I was treated with the highest regard by all levels of management, so I felt no bitterness about my departure. What company president allows an employee to take home his high-end sports car because the employee has a love of cars?!

- Frank DeGeorge

In talking with an employment practices attorney, I learned the reason most employees sue their employers was not because they were let go, rather their dismissal was a surprise. (breaking the Trust Towel rules).

Todd Welch

At Charter Partners, if our associates advance to better careers, we were successful. We want them to be where they want to be, and if it's with us, great. If it's with someone else, we will help them get there. We're looking for lifelong relationships. These trusted relationships allow people to recruit, hire, and train their replacements, beating the traditional two week's notice by a mile. Why can't everyone be like that? We think it's about trust, our third principle.

Principle #3: Trust

The Trust Principle comes last because it's the cleanup hitter of Cooperative Entrepreneurship. Both the Think and Team Principles are ineffective without trust. The Think Principle requires you trust your own ideas. Without trust, ideas can never manifest. Without trust, the Team Principle is only a group of individuals that happen to be working at the same time. Successful teams do not  exist without trust. Cooperative Entrepreneurship thrives in an environment of trust and sharing, but withers under protectionism and greed.

Trust is why your customers buy, your employees work, your suppliers supply, your insurers insure, and your bankers bank with you. You may excel at service, price, or possess valuable knowledge, but the bottom line why you're still in business comes from trust. Customers are like democracies: they vote with their money, and if you lose their trust, they'll take their vote elsewhere.

Trust is not easy to get, nor easy to keep. It's a complex concept full of dichotomy. For example, there is nothing in this world more solid than trust, as often symbolized by a stone. Yet, few things are softer or more

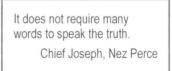

It does not require many words to speak the truth.

Chief Joseph, Nez Perce

ambiguous. We all know trust, but few good words exist to define it. Trust is universally recognized yet not generally practiced. Everyone has trust experience, but no one is an expert—yet.

Trust allows Cooperative Entrepreneurship to work. It multiplies your influence exponentially (expandable). Trust enables Cooperative Entrepreneurship to a form a river of innovation in place of the previous trickle.

In a fast-moving world, integrity and trust spawn a massive competitive advantage. Together they enable teams to make rapid decisions without the need for a legal contract every time someone tries to make a decision. What's more, trust and integrity enhance creativity, build teamwork, reduce unnecessary transactional costs (like memos to protect oneself), and make the relationship more fun, creating something new we could not have created alone.

Question:

Isn't this really just kumbaya?

Who doesn't want trust? It's something we all want. But let's be clear: entrepreurs are here to bring forth new innovations from the universe, and we need trust, something that requires hard work. Our kind of trust is used to faciligrate action for the purpose of co-creation. We're doing something together we could not have done alone and will not do with just anyone.

In 2008, I had the honor of meeting Russell Akoff. He has written dozens of management books and is Professor Emeritus of Management Science at the Wharton School of the University of Pennsylvania. We discussed focusing on trust as a core management tool. Russ challenged me to consider whether trust can stand by itself, meaning that trust is a result of a project, not the purpose of it. I concluded that trust needs to be treated as a verb. Trust, combined with innovative teams, significantly improves performance in almost every area you can measure. Trust is more than just the "right thing" or a "feel good." It is a competitive advantage over those who do not understand it's power. Cooperative Entrepreneurship uses trust as a tool to enhance success.

Question:

How do I trust in a world full of corruption?

Cooperative Entrepreneurship organizes a peer-selected group of successful entrepreneurs into a powerful economic community. This community intentionally uses trust as a tool to create success for everyone. The culture of trust acts like a membrane around a cell, providing a first line of defense against dangerous elements. If these elements get through to the body of the cell, the entire community goes to battle.

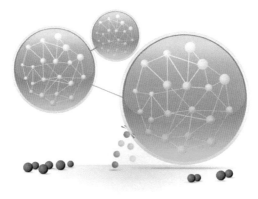

We DO NOT advocate blind trust. Our world comes with much risk of betrayal. You've read about our betrayals, and I'm sure you've experienced your own. Every day, the news runs stories about the pain caused by betrayal. We've witnessed how quickly organizations disappear when trust is broken: Enron, Worldcom, and Bernie Madoff to name a few.

The Trust Principle is integral to Cooperative Entrepreneurship. During the 15 years we've focused on trust, the world has lost more trust than at any other time in recent history. Everyone seems to wonder where it went and how to get it back.

Definition of Corruption
The misuse of entrusted power for private gain.

Talking about trust helps, but we need ways to measure it and tools to enhance it. Until now, few, if any, good ways existed to measure trust. In the next chapter, I'll introduce you to three tools to help you measure and develop trust in your business and your life.

Lessons Learned:

1. Love and passion drive innovation.

2. Everyone can be entrepreneurial.

3. A team can innovate better and faster than an individual.

4. Once a team has developed trust in each other they have a relationship for life.

5. Trust is the cornerstone for CE.

6. CE insulates you from corruption.

Tools for (it)

6

When my father identified trust as a major problem, we focused our energy on developing tools to nurture trust in our ourselves and our partners. First, we developed the Trust Towel as a way to build a common culture within our groups. Next we created a new way to measure trust called the Trust Scale with it's sister scale the Acceptable Variation of Trust (AVOT). The Trust Scale is the most comprehensive and where we will spend most of our focus.

This scale was co-created with Robert Porter Lynch who spent a summer at Charter Farms writing and helping to set the foundation for this book. As happens so often in entrepreneurship, we accidently discovered the Trust Scale in the process.

I was struggling with my project to find positive icons to balance off the negative icons on the Trust Towel. Robert and I ranked these behaviors from worst to first. When we saw the results it became obvious that we had a new powerful tool that for the first time, could rank our relationships with others.

The Trust Scale represents trust as a spectrum ranging from severe distrust to highly committed trust. Many personal and corporate relationships devolve into relative obscurity because the participants do not have architecture to design trust into their relationships.

At the high end of the Trust Scale are trusting relationships called Builders. Hopefully, you have experienced similar relationships that are highly cooperative, like family, friends, or playing on a sports team. At times, you shared material possessions or your deepest emotional senses with a loved one. Some people reach this highest form of trust when they engage in the synergistic[10] process of co-creation.

At the low end of the Trust Scale are distrustful relationships called Busters. This zone represents the type of situation where people attack one another, verbally or physically. They may also manipulate and deceive, often people retaliate with equally or more intense forms of distrustful behavior, spiraling into Annihilation on the Trust Scale.

The Trust Scale works because we're always moving up or down the spectrum. By identifying on the scale where you are in a relationship, you'll be better prepared to understand the actions and reactions of others.

---

[10] from the Greek: Syn – to join, and Energos – energies

BUILDERS TRUST SCALE

Creationship — 5

Partnership — 4

Friendship — 3

Guardianship — 2

Relationship — 1

E N C O U N T E R   0   E N C O U N T E R

-1

-2 Protection

-3 Manipulation

-4 Aggression

-5 Nullification

Annihilation

CHARTER PARTNERS
The Power of Mutual Friendship

CO-CREATED BY TODD WELCH AND ROBERT PORTER LYNCH
© 2008 TRUSTTOUR.COM AND CHARTER PARTNERS

BUSTERS

Question:

Why would we want to measure trust?

Soon after creating the Trust Scale I had an opportunity to understand how valuable it could be. My sister called and we agreed to share a pizza at my home. Planning to meet in half an hour, I left Charter Farms with my convertible roof down and my golden retriever, Nicky. I called in an order to Rocco's, a pizza shop in town, for pizza and salads.

To understand what happened next, you need to know that Nicky was a puppy from the Seeing Eye 4-H Club. Our job was to raise him until he was two and prepare him for his formal training as a guide dog for a visually impaired person. We were told to expose him to as many different environments as possible: airports, malls, restaurants, work, and even movies.

So here Nicky and I are, riding in the convertible, listening to music, with our hair blowing in the wind (well truth be told, his hair and the fuzz that is left on top of my head). When we reach Rocco's, I get Nicky out of the car and head into the shop, expecting to expose him to  another new situation. As I moved through the doors and towards the front counter, Nicky in tow, I immediately noticed the disturbed look on the face of the person behind the counter.

I gave my last name and asked if my order was ready. Based on the staffs' expression, I explained that the dog was a puppy training to be a guide dog. I asked if it was OK that he was with me. The man behind the counter said, "Your pizza is not ready. Please remove the dog from the shop." Again, I tried to explain that Nicky was in training, but he shook his head and pointed to the door. Feeling somewhat humiliated, I turned around, walked through the double set of doors, and stood outside to wait for my pizza.

Standing next to the highway, holding Nicky, my frustration increased as the minutes ticked away. I poked my head in the door, "Pizza ready yet?" "No, not yet," he said. After 10 more minutes, and using the Three No's Rule, I tried again. I poked my head in and asked if it was okay to put Nicky in the vestibule area while we waited. This way he stayed out of the main restaurant and harm's way next to the busy highway. "No!" was the answer.

The Three No's Rule

When trying to convince someone about your idea, a no is not a no unless they've said it three times.

Scott Welch

Cars continued to whiz by, and my frustration got the better of me. Deciding I wouldn't deal with this situation any longer, I told the counter guy I could not wait and was leaving. He looked surprised and threw up his hands. Later, I learned I had walked out on Rocco himself.

Nicky and I got back in the car. I called another pizza shop with delivery service and ordered the same thing. After being told delivery would take 45 minutes, I agreed and drove home mumbling under my breath that I was never going back to Rocco's again. Rocco was stuck with a pizza and salads, I was stuck waiting another 45 minutes to have dinner with my family, and Nicky was stressed out. I assumed Rocco didn't care about my business, my dog, or my predicament. It was a bad situation for everyone.

This is when I thought about the Trust Scale and realized I was having an Encounter and hoping to build a Relationship, but Rocco was immediately into Protection and my response was to move to Nullifcation.

I later went back to talk with Rocco about the experience. I offered to pay for the pizza, which he refused. I then asked him what his experience was like. He explained that the health inspector is very serious about his job and often went over the pizza shop with a fine-tooth comb. Rocco was concerned the dog would be a major violation and the inspector could shut down his business or fine him. He also shared the story about a time he allowed a dog into the shop and found a "present" under the table. He didn't need this kind of disrespect. Rocco went on to say that if he'd known I was outside holding the dog he would have brought the pizza out to us. We agreed we both made assumptions without fully understanding each other's situation. Now we had built a Relationship on the Trust Scale.

This scenario plays out millions of times every day—people protecting themselves and hurting each other in the process. By using the Trust Scale we can do better.

The Trust Scale

Now that you understand the basics, I am going to let Robert explain the specifics of how the scale can be used. I will be back to introduce you to Acceptable Variations of Trust (AVOT).

Encounter—Neutral:

We'll start at the center. Encounter is the starting point of trust. Encounter represents a first meeting with no real judgment, good or bad, of the experience. The first time you go to a new pizza place, pay an attendant at a parking garage, or meet a potential business partner is an encounter. You could define it as any transaction or exchange. Can you remember the name or face of the toll-booth attendant? Probably not, since you had a transactional encounter based on a simple exchange. There was sufficient trust to do the exchange, but, if significant money were at stake, you'd want both the safety and security of a strong relationship.

When shopping, we put enough trust in the brand, or the store's reputation, to complete the exchange of goods or services for money, but not enough trust to engage in a deeper relationship.

Trust Builders

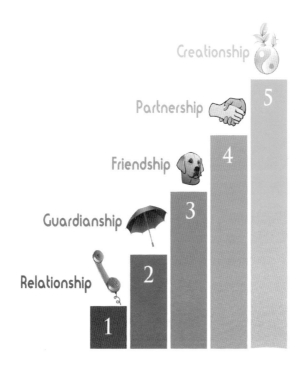

Creationship

Partnership

Friendship

Guardianship

Relationship

1 2 3 4 5

Relationship

Have you ever look up the definition of "relationship" in *Webster's Dictionary*? The obscure definition will shock you: "to be related." No wonder we're so poor at forming relationships. We don't even know what we're talking about! We can't even define what we mean by a relationship, what we want in a relationship, or how relationships function.

To build a relationship, the other person needs to know you're listening, without judgment. Communication/ Assumption illustrates the difference between judgmental listening and listening to build a relationship. When we listen with compassion, learning, and constructive inquiry, we begin to build trust. People feel like they are receiving *support*.

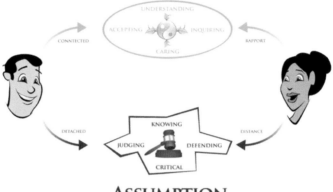

Listening and inquiring with interest and compassion means starting without assumptions or expectations. Assumptions and expectations impair our ability to see reality. If you respond with criticism, judgment, and defensiveness, the other person's immediate reaction is to defend, counter-attack, or blame. Don't fall in this trap, because it will send the relationship into the distrust death spiral.

When the other person is blaming, judgmental, and critical, you might suggest that they are not providing the responses that will build trust or a productive relationship. Be an inspiration that doesn't tolerate abusiveness or unreasonableness. Continue to ask open, non-judgmental questions. These are far more important than demonstrating that you have all the answers. Making demands or criticizing won't draw in people like curiosity and being open to discovery.

When building a trusting relationship, minimal boundary conditions must be satisfied, honored and respected by both parties. Other's count on you to understand personal interests, needs, and concerns, which gives the assurance that, ultimately, you can be trusted. Without this assurance, the relationship is broken, and you've fallen below the line into distrust.

 G U A R D I A N S H I P   The next level of trust provides *safety* and *security* to the other person. (This level may embrace the prior level, but goes a step further.) Guardianship can be one way, much like a parent with a child, but it can go both ways, too, in mutual guardianship, like soldiers on a battlefield. As an employer, every entrepreneur has a duty and responsibility, both morally and legally, to protect their employees' safety on the job, pay their unemployment taxes, protect their civil rights, and provide a harassment-free work environment. In return, you expect employees to maintain a Guardianship over the work place by not stealing, reporting hazards, improving your competitive advantage, and contributing to their teammates' well being.

Individuals who don't feel safe in your presence will be protective or fearful. Guardianship means knowing that you won't intentionally hurt me. At a deeper level, it's *reliance*. I know that:

- you'll be there to protect me from harm
- you'll be there when I need you
- you won't sacrifice me for self interest
- you'll protect my best interests as well as your own
- you won't be negligent
- we will protect each other's safety

At the Guardianship level, the issue of honor and integrity becomes critical to building trust. Beyond respect, Guardianship means honoring your essence and defending you from attack. Others expect the same from you.

For this level of trust, we use a dog as the symbol. Why? After 10,000 years of selective breeding that started with a wolf, we're left with dogs who give us what we want in humans but can't seem to get. Ask any dog owner what they like in their dog. Typical answers include: he's always there for me, always happy to see me, loyal, faithful, and protective, never carries a grudge or the baggage of unfulfilled expectations, playful, and makes me smile.

> The language of friendship is not words but meanings
>
> Thoreau

In other words, the very qualities we wish we experienced in other people! Dogs are often more trusting and trusted than people. (Should we be more like dogs?)

> Friendship is composed of a single soul inhabiting two bodies.
>
> He who hath many friends hath none.
>
> Aristotle

When we build trust at the friendship level, we embrace all the prior levels of trust, but add some very energizing and vital creative forces to the relationship.

Friendship also implies a playfulness that brings out our inner child. This playfulness brings us back to days when we had fewer concerns about achievement or looking good. At this level of trust, we can let our egos melt away and engage more directly.

> To a friend's house, the way is never long.
>
> Viola Lynch

In a friendship, trust allows our goals and fears, our deepest yearnings and our personal limits/ failures to be put out in the open with no sense of diminishment. We're willing to be open and transparent with no hidden agendas because the trust is firm and strong.

> Trust the man who: lays down his self-interest for that of another, tells the truth when it's not to his advantage, and adheres to his values in times of chaos and strife.

Did you ever wonder why so many of us have so few real friends? You've heard the term "fair-weather friend," a person only around during the good times. But woe the day when you hit a personal crisis—a divorce, an illness, or a financial disaster —the presumed friend is gone with the wind. Unfortunately, you elevated the wrong relationship to the Friendship level.

 **Partnership**   A partnership respects and cherishes the different thinking and capabilities between two or more people or organizations. It's the synergy between various strengths and the alignment of common purposes that makes a partnership a true alliance. You see partnerships in business all the time. For example, one person does outside sales; another keeps the finances on track; another runs operations.

Based on our years of successful alliance formation, we know the level this takes is a step above the rest. Great partnering relationships require a number of things to make them work effectively:

Shared Vision

Where there is no vision, everything defaults to politics. While making a dollar is essential in business, great partnerships always synchronize their minds to the new opportunity. They have to pull in the same direction. The winds of change are always blowing, and, if you want to achieve your goal, you must share a common vision.

Shared Values

No legal agreement can make a partnership or alliance work. It must function because the parties can trust at the highest levels of integrity. Diminish the trust and the relationship rapidly deteriorates. Cooperative Entrepreneurs build their relationships on strong values that can withstand a rapidly changing world. For anyone who sails, we compare it to "anchoring to windward" so our bow stays headed in the right direction.

Shared Resources

Partnerships and alliances leverage their capabilities by sharing key assets such as technology, customer base, plant facilities, sales forces, and research. By sharing, the Cooperative Entrepreneur can leverage precious resources.

Shared Risk and Rewards

By sharing risk and reward, the partnership becomes a trust-building vehicle because people have "skin in the game." The more everyone shares risks and rewards, the more powerful the level of commitment. In business, your measurement system is one of the essential ingredients for success. Misaligned metrics cause dysfunctional actions, poor results, and ultimately distrust.

For this level of trust, we crafted a new word. Creationship meaning that we can do something extraordinary together that we can't do alone and will not do with just anyone. Virtually all the great discoveries and innovations in today's world are happening in this way. Industries and technologies are putting this force to work in science with the Watson-Crick discoveries of DNA or the

NASA teams sending a man to the moon. Take the Genomics Project as an example; it's the confluence between medicine, mathematics, informatics, and computers. Its goal was to identify all the approximately 20-25,000 genes in human DNA. Even your automobile benefits from Creationship. Today, 25-40% of your automobile's value comes from electronics, not mechanics. Just 25 years ago, the electronics value was only 1%.

A Creationship is the gold standard by which you can measure your ability to trust others and be trusted. It embraces the prior elements of trust building and then unleashes a connection between the hearts and minds of the co-creators with new ideas generating like spontaneous combustion. Cooperative Entrepreneurship is all about generating ideas that can be transformed into new value for an organization.

> We will create one minor invention every 10 days, and a Big One every six months.
>
> -- Thomas Edison to his invention team at Menlo Park, 1872

Purpose and Destiny

Some of the most co-creative people on the planet have a deep sense of personal purpose or destiny; they know why they are on this earth. Purpose gives meaning and value to what we do, a reason for being. Destiny means we aim our purpose higher, to achieve something worthy of our collective effort, something we and our children can be proud of. To accomplish this mission, we must engage others. If you have one or more of these rare people in your organization, nurture them.

No Judgment

The most important thing an entrepreneur can do to build a trustworthy innovation engine is to create a company culture that encourages innovation day in and day out. In Creationship, you focus metrics and rewards on Cooperative Entrepreneurship, not only on people working independently.

Cherish and Synergize Differences

It's been said that we build communities with people who are similar, but learn from people who are different. The Cooperative Entrepreneur's task is to join these two forces together. Cherishing the differences and building a fellowship that thrives on differences in thinking are necessary for innovation.

Laugh

Creationship is not all-grinding labor. Co-creative teams have fun at what they do and laugh a lot. Research shows that laughter releases endorphins that trigger creativity. When people laugh, they are spontaneously creating magical moments.

Most everyone has enjoyed the magic of a Rogers and Hammerstein musical. These musicals did not, however, only focus on happiness. They also had a deeper purpose, highlighting timely, powerful issues, like the role of women, racism, violence, and dictatorships. But it wasn't easy. Oscar Hammerstein was considered a failure when he first teamed with Richard Rogers. However, they had the right chemistry to produce majestic and magical music. Their very close relationship brought out the best in each other with mutual inspiration.

> In everyone's life at some time, our inner fire goes out. It is then burst into flame by an encounter with another human being. We should all be thankful for those people who rekindle the inner spirit.
>
> Albert Schweitzer

Trust Busters

The multiple ways we've learned to "bust trust" are so well defined in our society they should be considered an art form. Take the legal profession; they have made an entire economic system out of distrust, both creating it and protecting their clients from the harm of distrust. Many professional labor and procurement negotiators are in the business of squeezing the other side, creating enormous amounts of distrust.

Below we outline the levels of distrust so that you can identify and talk about what type of distrust exists when it manifests. In this way, by having a common *language* (words and pictures) and *architecture* (framework) you can discuss in vivid detail your experiences.

We've found that when you have a mental picture of what happens in the distrust zone, you then have a way to bring the behaviors out in the open. Here's a brief description of these trust busters (there are more than these five, but these are the most prevalent):

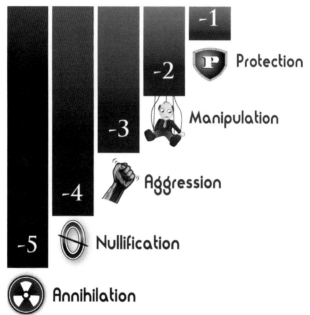

 **Protection** typically takes two forms, active and passive. Active protectors often hide behind mountains of legal agreements, non-disclosures, and red tape. Over protectiveness often creates the distrust from which they attempt to protect themselves.

Passive protectors withdraw, flee, hide, or remain silent, making no commitments, avoiding interactions, and taking no risks. Bureaucrats are professional protectors, deflecting responsibility with obscure rules, convoluted processes, and abstract reasoning.

Sometimes, there's a need for Protection when your honor or dignity is at risk. You must also protect yourself from physical, mental and financial attacks. Protection makes sense when you're facing corruption, and you need to stay strong through a storm to fight another day.

Protection is the only defense that the most trustful of us has against corruption. Ghandi and Martin Luther King used Protection against their persecutors, but they never went into the darker uses of trust busters. As a Cooperative Entrepreneur you mustn't descend any lower and only go to Protection when you're attacked.

 **MaNipulatiON**

The mind of the manipulator has determined they cannot expect the world to respond in predictable and reasonable ways. So they trick the world to their advantage because the lack of trust does not allow it to respond predictably. (This rationale obviously sets up a circular, self-fulfilling prophesy.)

The most recognized manipulation game is whining or complaining. Such games attack others by focusing attention on how everyone else is wrong, bad, guilty, or incompetent. The whiner seeks to get his own way by maneuvering others into the "bad guy" role, often getting away with it because placating is easier than establishing more trusting roles.

Surprises are one of the other ways the manipulator operates. Sometimes the surprise is innocent, but surprises come from self-interest that fails to take others into consideration. In a sense, a surprise implies you don't exist or weren't important enough to the manipulator to consider. Our response may be to "get them back" by out-manipulating the manipulator, or perhaps by playing people against one another.

 Aggression uses someone's power to threaten you. Often taking the form of a game, the aggressive person believes the best defense is a good offense and takes the initiative to demonstrate superiority, strength, and power. Aggression can take the form of a big ego to disguise a sense of insecurity. Insecure egoists will destroy trust by always putting themselves and their agenda first.

Aggressors will bellow and bluster their way through or into any situation, always looking out for themselves. To demonstrate their power, they'll play power games—sitting higher than you at a meeting, telling stories about their aggressiveness, speaking crassly in public, or insisting their answer is the only right one. For them, the only way is their way; "he who has the gold, rules."

Passive-aggressive behavior is yet another game some play. Since outright aggression is a trickier game, being passive aggressive allows one to obstruct others by acting helpless, procrastinating, becoming upset, displaying hurt feelings, resenting others, or refusing to act after multiple requests. You're meant to think things are all right, but these subtle tricks often confuse and hurt.

Sometimes the passive-aggressive person develops such a habitual use of this trick they no longer recognize the behavior. For example, the passive-aggressive might be habitually late to anything they don't want to engage in. Beware of the passive-aggressor. Usually intelligent and outwardly successful, these individuals observe your behavior, looking for cracks. They see you as a threat to their position as the best, most powerful, or smartest.

Nullification

Have you ever been shunted aside, zeroed out, made meaningless, or marginalized? That's Nullification, and it's not pretty. When someone walks out on you or ignores you, you're being nullified.

Many religious groups use this technique to ostracize rule breakers; Catholics can be excommunicated, Jehovah's Witnesses can be disfellowshipped; other sects call it shunning.

Nullification can happen passively when others fail to respond to you in a meeting or to your request for assistance. To illustrate the power of Nullification, studies have shown that it's more damaging to neglect an infant than to show violence. Nullification is destructive because it thwarts a vital desire in everyone: the need to be needed and the need to make a difference.

Annihilation

Annihilation destroys a relationship and everything associated with it. It intends to wipe you off the map. Where Nullification pretends you don't exist, Annihilation is the action that wants you removed from the environment. Words like destruction and obliteration come to mind. In order to get to Annihilation, there must be many miscommunications and the perception of betrayal. Watch what happens when you ask anyone if they've been betrayed. Usually it's a reaction of emotional pain. Everyone has their stories, and their pain associated with the betrayal. Their hurt is carried around like a private wound, often with guarded silence. Other's turn betrayal into blame or worse, revenge.

Greek literature and Roman history are filled with many stories of betrayal. At the end of the middle ages, Machiavelli wrote his famous advice to his reigning prince for combating a society filled with betrayal. Shakespeare, writing four hundred years ago, described Brutus's betrayal of Caesar with the famous line:

How many ages hence shall this ... be acted over in states unborn and accents yet unknown!

In America, the names Benedict Arnold, Lee Harvey Oswald, or Richard Nixon are immediately associated with betrayal.

Purposeful betrayal is all too common in our daily world. Its corrosive force destroys teamwork, co-creativity, and spiritual community. In response to betrayal, people typically withdraw into a protective cocoon. Others react the opposite, fighting with a vengeful energy that leaves no possibility of reconciliation. When done unintentionally, betrayal takes a variety of forms—selfishness or insecurity—often manifesting as creeping dissent, an angst of complaint, blame, undermining, resentment, negativity, fault-finding, character assassination, and endless complaints.

When this behavior occurs at work, daily routine becomes nothing more than bittersweet travail with neither victory nor valor, nor honor, nor heroics. In the family, betrayals ultimately lead to divorce, delinquency, despondency, depression, destructive revenge, or even death.

When done intentionally, the result is usually far more insidious, destructive, and often horrifying. If the ghosts of archetypical betrayal are prolific in your organization, look to the top where their spirit may reside. And also look within to see if you are trapped in a culture of intrigue, innuendo, and doubt in which you've become one of the principal or supporting actors.

Using the Trust Scale

To make the most effective use of the Trust Scale, just discuss with another person where your relationship exists now on the scale (it can exist on multiple points), and where you want it to go. Often you may have higher (or lower) expectations than another person. Then discuss what has to change to put things in the zone where you mutually agree the relationship can maximize its potential.

Trust is a Choice

How much trust exists between people is a choice we make. However, most people make the choice reactively or subconsciously, without discussion or interactive design. This mistake has kept relationships—personal, organizationally, and even internationally—stuck in distrust.

The level of trust that exists in any relationship is a *mutual choice*. Building trust should not be something that happens reactively, thoughtlessly, or invisibly. Trust is most powerful when it's the result of an active choice determined by how you want the world to work. For example, suppose a fellow businessperson betrayed you. While you may think you had no choice, the person who betrayed you did have a choice:

- *Intentionally* or *Maliciously*—It was done after some deliberation or desire to hurt or harm you.

- *Unconsciously* or *Negligently*—Their mind made a choice to repress any consideration for their motive, action, or its consequences.

- *Reactively*—The choice was triggered and driven by emotions, not rational thought.

Also consider that you may have created conditions that drove their choice, made it easier, or because they expected no dire consequences for the betrayal.

Thank you Robert, and now on to AVOT.

Question:

Where does trust start?

Trust starts with you. How often do you tell the truth? According to Dan Ariely, professor of behavioral economics at Duke University and head of the eRationality research group at MIT, people will cheat moderately given the opportunity. It turns out that many of us will take that pen from the office or a towel from the hotel, and not tell the whole truth.

It's been my experience that most of us do not tell major lies. These would violate our integrity. Small lies, however, feel reasonable and, maybe, even necessary in our lives. These small violations of trust are within the comfort zone or our Acceptable Variation of Trust (AVOT). We don't feel that these small infractions materially impact our integrity. But in reality they are the small cracks that lead to even larger variations.

Violations of integrity happen more frequently and more severely when the environment or culture encourages it. For example, *Wall Street Journal* reporters Peggy Chaudhry and Stephen A. Stumpf found that consumers in Brazil, India, and the U.S., said consumption of fake pharmaceuticals was an unethical behavior.[11] In Russia and China, it was not important at all. In these two countries, consumers would buy the fake pharmaceuticals even if they realized it was an immoral or illegal act. Is it a coincidence that countries that have high corruption rates have people that act that way individually? AVOT varies from one family to another, one business to another and one country to another

---

11 "Real About Fakes," *The Wall Street Journal*

Leadership is the key. If our family members or business associates violate trust, but the leader does not punish them, or worse they are rewarded, then both frequency and severity increase. This behavior changes the game for everyone. People start to think they need to cheat to win, starting an ugly cycle of deepening mistrust.

Anne Baum, a business consultant and adjunct professor at DeSales University was the first person to introduce me to the idea that *assumption* is one of the great contributors to mistrust. When Anne asks her MBA students, "What are the most important characteristics of a leader?" they respond with, "visionary," "charismatic," or "team-builder." She then suggests the best answer is "integrity." Anne and her partner Elmer Gates, former CEO Fuller Co. often get pushback, because most people in the class believe you cannot reach senior levels of leadership if you don't cheat. Anne and Elmer then spend the next 12 weeks trying to unwind that mindset.

Another example of AVOT involves the recent mortgage crisis where mortgages were sold on undervalued properties to people with poor credit histories. Few would say this was a good business practice, but, in the short run, mortgage companies and banks made great returns, and managers were showered with promotions, praise, and money. Thousands followed suit. Even those who did not believe in the philosophy got caught up playing the game to keep up with the returns. While not illegal, the behavior was hardly moral. I'm confident that the people involved knew they had crossed the integrity line, but many convinced themselves this was an Acceptable Variation of Trust.

What happens when a critical mass of companies act this way? Could events spiral into a monster and put our economy at risk? If we want to prevent a similar situation in the future, we need to examine our own AVOT. When we give in to a culture of trust variations, we start to kill each other, financially, socially, and spiritually. The solution starts with you.

It may help to look at a variation of the Trust Scale that can help to define your AVOT. Find the range that represents you. For example, some of the worst villains of our time would fit in the A range; some of our heroes would fit into the E range. Most of us would fit somewhere in between. It seems obvious to me that to be a Cooperative Entrepreneur you have to constantly work at maintaining an AVOT in the E range. What is your personal AVOT what is your companies?

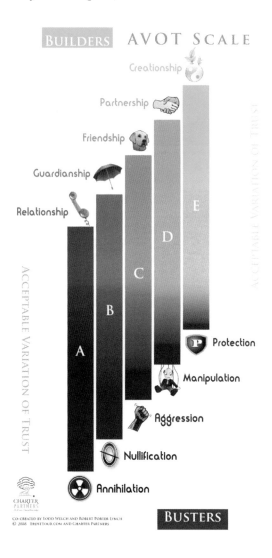

Question:

How do I improve my AVOT?

Wristbands that promote awareness for cancer and other good causes have become very popular. I believe that trust fits in with the most important concerns in the world and I'd like to introduce the Trust Band. I realize by doing this, I risk trivializing trust but I found it to be just the opposite and use it as an effective tool. I have used it to remind myself of my own zero tolerance policy and it helps me keep my AVOT in the E range. Here is how we use the Trust Band to increase our AVOT.

TRUST BAND

The concept is simple. When you are being trustful you wear it green side up, and when you have busted someone's trust you flip it to the red side. When you reestablish the trust, you can turn the band back to green. I find myself getting uncomfortable wearing the red side up for any extended amount of time providing a sense of urgency to repair trust.

My first experience with the Trust Band happened on a busy Saturday night in Cape May. At one of my family's favorite restaurants, eight of us gathered to celebrate Dad's birthday. I called ahead for a reservation, when I got there a crowd stood around the podium and it took 10 minutes to reach the hostess.

She greeted me and asked, "Is your whole party here?" I hesitated. Dad and Mom hadn't arrived, but I knew she would not seat us until our "whole party" was there and I didn't want to wade back through the crowd again. So, I said, "Yes they are." She smiled and said she would seat us. As I went to gather everyone, I remembered the Trust Band! I'd lied. It was a little lie, and I thought, "No harm, no foul." It was in my Acceptable Variation of Trust . . . ugh! I turned on my heel and told the hostess that two people were still missing from our party. She smiled again, and said, "No problem we will seat you anyway."

Lessons Learned:

1. There is a way to measure trust.
2. Communication builds trust.
3. Assumption destroys trust.
4. Each of us has a variation in integrity (AVOT).
5. The larger the variation, the more Corruption.
6. A Cooperative Entrepreneur works to collaborate with others who are working toward higher integrity.
7. When you tell the truth, you might still get seated.
8. A physical symbol can act as a reminder to stay in your integrity.

We have combined the thoughts from the Trust Scale with those of AVOT to capture in a graphic everything you've learned in this chapter. This final version of the Trust Scale can be used both as a measurement of your relationships and your personal AVOT.

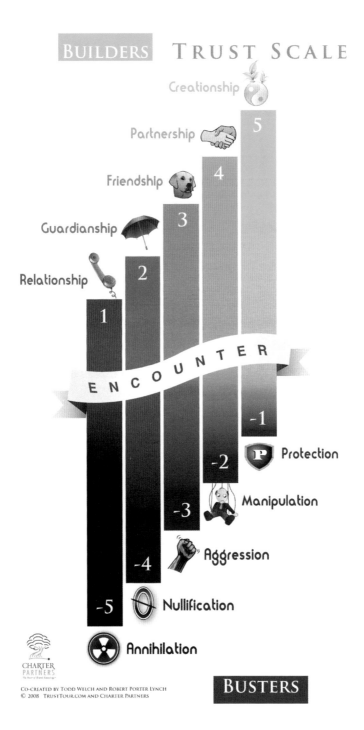

BUILDERS TRUST SCALE

Creationship

Partnership — 5

Friendship — 4

Guardianship — 3

Relationship — 2

1

ENCOUNTER

-1

P Protection

-2

Manipulation

-3

Aggression

-4

-5 Nullification

Annihilation

CHARTER PARTNERS

CO-CREATED BY TODD WELCH AND ROBERT PORTER LYNCH
© 2008 TRUSTTOUR.COM AND CHARTER PARTNERS

BUSTERS

You Can Do it 7

Greed is good
- Gordon Gekko (Wall Street)

In CE "NEED" is good. We're looking for answers to the needs of people. We intend to find a way to fill these needs through honest collaboration. What could be more important in business than making the world better for you being here (Think Principle)? Does anything rank higher than doing good with other people (Team Principle)? Does another way exist to do it than honestly (Trust Principle)?

You CAN do it, I know so because I've done it, as have many of my partners. Besides being new, and even uncomfortable, it's not easy. Like anything new, there's risk and reward. I can tell you that it's a better way to do business, but we've still much to learn. I don't have all the answers, and you'll decide the value for yourself once you try it.

Now let's walk through the three-step process to start you as a Cooperative Entrepreneur. Remember, CE is a way of thinking and acting. Like the creative process, no hard rules exist. Since I have a good deal of experience, I believe I can provide you with some guidance so you don't make unnecessary mistakes. Below are three rules to keep you on track as you start doing 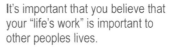. At the end of each step, you'll take a short test to make sure you're ready to move to the next step. A quick note: when putting together a new gadget, most people will try to assemble the parts freestyle, reading the directions only when something goes wrong. With this in mind, I present these steps and trust you to put them to their best use:

1.   Leading with Honest Purpose

2.   Creating a Vision for CE

3.   Taking a Risk to start CE

Step #1: Leading with Honest Purpose

I've had the honor to participate on multiple leadership panels. After one event, a young man raised his hand and asked the classic leadership question:

"Mr. Welch, are leaders made, or are leaders born?"

At that time, my best answer was BOTH, and that's what I told him. I realize I was only partially right. There is a better answer. Like trust, **leadership *is a choice***. Leadership is something you decide by yourself for yourself.

In this same meeting, I heard one of my peers say the other classic statement, "You're not a leader unless someone is following you." It's hard not to agree with that definition, but as I thought about it, I see another side. In my experience, I was the hardest person I had to convince to follow me. I had to trust myself. Trust that I knew enough to get started, that I saw the problem clearly, that I could learn and adapt as we progressed. If

> It's important that you believe that your "life's work" is important to other peoples lives.
>
> Scott Welch

I could accomplish that, then I had a chance of getting others to follow me.

I bring this up because if is going to take hold, it has to start with me, then you, then others. I wrote this book trusting that everything I have been through, everything I have learned is for a reason. I believe the reason I discovered Cooperative Entrepreneurship is that it's a better answer to a better future.

You've had chances to lead in the past. Maybe you took them, maybe you didn't. Choosing to lead is a very personal decision. If you're not able to lead, you can still join a team and do your best. If you are able to lead, join me and know that you are not alone.

I have made my choice: I am choosing to lead as a Cooperative Entrepreneur because I love it, I know it, and I believe in it. Being a CE will make me a better person and the world a better place. Together we can lead people to a new and better way of doing business.

Question:

Where does leadership start?

The primary role of a leader, after they set the vision, is to create trust with everyone—employees, vendors, suppliers, customers, and alliance members—in the network. Thomas Edison said, "Before work is started there must be forethought, systems planning, intelligence and most importantly *honest purpose.*" Why are you leading? Does your agenda focus on you, your ego, your control, your money, and your success? Or, does your agenda show balance, focusing on worthwhile projects, solving problems, and building an organization that does the right thing and creates value for yourself and others?

How does anyone know when the balance between self-interest and the greater good is right? If people focus only on the greater good, they don't satisfy their own needs. Communism tried to focus on the greater good and ended up serving neither the greater good nor an individual's needs. When we start with Honest Purpose, we do the right things for the right reasons. Honor is the means, and Purpose is the ends. Honest Purpose means we think consciously about balancing our own personal self-interest with the needs of others in our realm of influence.

Cooperative Entrepreneurship requires the foundational principle of Honest Purpose. In the long run, neither internal teams nor other businesses will work with you without a bond of trust.

When an entrepreneur focuses on Honest Purpose the critical issue is not, "Will I be successful?", but "What service or value will my company provide to others?" The far more important goal to meet clients' needs honestly and purposefully comes first. It may surprise many that most entrepreneurs don't start their businesses primarily to make money; rather it is to control their destiny. At this decision point, every entrepreneur must face the issue of Honest Purpose.

When a company purposefully produces inferior, dangerous products or makes unsustainable claims, then it violates the standard of Honest Purpose. Eventually trust will erode in the eyes of its clients; its brands will become worthless and no amount of advertising will be the cure.

Far from easy, Honest Purpose can be especially hard to hold onto when you live paycheck to paycheck or with no paycheck at all. When we talk about survival, our AVOT begins to stretch, and we're tempted to resort to tools like manipulation and aggression to achieve our goals. We all have to make money, but we face a paradox. In the long run, we can make much more by holding on to our integrity versus making short-term compromises.

You have now been exposed to the available Trust Tools: the Trust Towel, the Trust Scale, the Trust Bands, and the AVOT. There's a high probability you're an intelligent, honest leader already. However, a tiny crack in your wall of personal integrity can destroy everything. Sorely missing in today's environment is the desire to take personal responsibility for ourselves. It is for this reason, that we take yet another step deeper into trust.

> **Definition of corruption**:
> The misuse of entrusted power.
>
> **Definition of integrity:**
> Confidence a person has in being who they are inside and out.

I am not suggesting you need to be perfect. I know that I'm not perfect, and so I always work on my personal integrity. Trust requires conscious practice. We all carry vulnerabilities hidden away until we're under pressure. Under pressure, anyone, including me and you, might abandon our values and fall prey to corruption. Many a great leader has fallen prey to this vulnerability.

You need to know about the potential for cracks because if Cooperative Entrepreneurship lacks integrity, you can hurt yourself, your family, and your business. Lack of integrity can

> "I'm not upset that you lied to me, I'm upset that from now on I can't believe you"
>
> Friedrich Nietzsche

spread to other team members like a virus, taking down the whole group. That's why we're so serious about trust.

Trust Test - Personal Integrity

Ask yourself this Trust Test question. Only you can answer it, and only you can grade your response. You are the only person that will ever know if you were honest. You are the only person that can graduate yourself to the next test.

Question:

Am I willing to make a commitment to personal integrity?

☐ **NO**. Thank you for your honesty! That's the first step. If you want to come back in the future, we are here for you.

☐ **YES.** Ok great, there is more work ahead. Lets get started with your vision.

Step # 2: Create a Vision

Question:

What does the future look like?

A vision gives our minds a starting place to approach a problem or opportunity. It creates mental space for you and your team to work. Vision creates something from nothing and enables you to disrupt the flow of everything in your path in the name of progress. All the great leaders have vision. They cause revolutions, change our lives forever, and we love them for it. You probably know a few of these guys:

Henry Ford "automobile for everyone"

Wright Brothers "we can fly"

Thomas Edison "light the world"

Walt Disney "laughter of every child"

Bill Gates "computer on every desk"

Google Guys "organize the world's info "

Walt Disney loved to spend time with his two daughters. On Sundays, he took them to the carnival. They always had a great time, but as he watched the girls on the merry-go-round, he thought things could be better. The rides were designed for children and parents couldn't participate with their kids. Additionally, these rides were transient and not always safe. The carnival site was generally dirty and the attendants were not very friendly. Walt knew he could do better.

Walt saw a different future.

- What if he could create a place where families could enjoy the rides together?

- What if the rides were both entertaining and educational?

- What if everyone that worked there was friendly and the place was spotless?

Disneyland was introduced to the world as an innovation of epic proportions.

Dan Rogers, a world class hiker and author of *America One Step at a Time*, told me how he has logged over 10,000 miles hiking America. He hiked north to south, east to west, and from a place we don't get to see very often . . . inside. Dan's vision was to walk across America, and he celebrated his small wins along the way. Starting from his front porch, he danced on the county line 12 miles later, 200 miles more, he danced on the state line, and 3,400 miles later, he danced on the beach at the Pacific Ocean. After hearing his story, I suggested that his vision had set in motion some creative tension that allowed him to innovate and overcome obstacles to reach his goal. He agreed, mentioning that his backpack lost 20 pounds along the way, a necessity that he innovated one ounce at a time.

> Our only real security lies in our collective ability to invent the future.
>
> Todd Welch

Dan told me he's hiked both alone and on a team, "When you are alone there is no room for error. If you only have enough food and water for a section of the hike, but have underestimated the distance, you're on your own. If you are with a team, you have a better chance of both estimating the distance correctly and sharing resources along the way." Dan noted that on the trail there is an ability to build trust quickly, noting all have a common mission, the stakes are high, and you're spending sustained time together.

Question:

How do you know when you've lost your vision?

Think about it — Dan says, "If someone asked you to dig ditches and at the end of the week pays you a box of plastic pink flamingos, would you do it? Probably not." But every day, we take our hard-earned money into the store and buy useless stuff.

Recently I was traveling from my regional airport and had a good laugh wondering why 25 plastic pink flamingos adorned the main entrance sign. One more tip from Dan: "Think cost per mile when buying a pair of shoes; the cheapest might actually be the most expensive."

Dan's leadership philosophy is Go With The Flow or (G)oal, (W)in, (T)rust, and (F)ellowship. When I thought about this philosophy and how I would apply it to business, the first three seemed obvious, but I asked Dan to explain the importance of fellowship? Dan explained, "When you see a beautiful sunset and say out loud, 'Wow that's a beautiful sunset,' but no one is there to answer, you know how important fellowship is to your life." He continued, "Why leave that part of the human experience at home when you go to work?" Good point.

What is it that you can make better? What is it that you should be leading? What is it that you know you can do, but haven't had the tools?

Question:

How do I create a culture that supports my vision?

We've talked a lot about the principles of Think, Team, and Trust. At times, we described them as independent components. But, like the elements of light, water, and soil in a biosphere, they are an integrated network of tools working in harmony, each element making the other exponentially more effective.

Innovation is the Holy Grail of Cooperative Entrepreneurship, but how do you achieve it consistently? Innovation happens many different ways: a person with brilliant insight; an accidental happening; a vision or a crisis that opens up new thinking. You hope these random experiences will occur, and you'll be ready to make the most of it. What if you could create a system that encourages a constant flow of new ideas on purpose? Cooperative Entrepreneurship creates this kind of system, enhancing the odds of repetitive innovative thinking. It also allows for the proofing of these ideas in a safe and non-judgmental environment.

An example of this culture can be found within the walls of Pixar Animation Studios, which I had the privilege to visit. You immediately feel surrounded by a culture of trust, respect, creativity, and pride. It is evident that diversity is valued. I saw that some of their best ideas came from people that did not fit the traditional mold. This respect for diversity allows for no single right way to achieve a result. In this type of world, people can be more creative, but one thing is for sure, none of us is as creative as all of us.

Question:

Why so much focus on my behavior?

Your vision can only be successful if the culture of the organization supports it. The culture is a reflection of the leader's actions. As an organization's leader, you're like a radio announcer. You need to be clear about two things. One is your message, and the second is the strength of the signal. If the message is clear from the announcer, and the radio frequency strong, then we call this integrity. If it's not clear, or strong, we get bled from other random stations. This leads to corruption, or lack of integrity. Your company culture will follow your lead based on the signal you send.

South Korea's past president, President Roh, committed suicide after accusations of taking a bribe while in office. Just before walking off a cliff near his home, he posted this quote on his website: "I no longer feel qualified to speak for things such as democracy, progressiveness and justice." I don't know if he did it because he was corrupt himself, or others were painting him as a corrupt person. Either way, his action is a graphic example of how deeply honor, integrity, and trust can affect the meaning of our lives.

Gandhi said, "My life is my message." What is your message? This clarity can make the difference between shouting your message from the top of the mountain or walking off the mountaintop.

Walt Disney once ordered figs for breakfast. Every member of his team in turn said they would have figs too. Walt, a man who loved originality, got upset, stood up, exclaiming, "Be an original!" That's a clear signal. Bill Gates' executive team adopted Bill's habit of rocking back and forth as they took their time to think. Quality thinking is highly valued at Microsoft. In Richard Nixon's memoirs he took responsibility for Watergate by admitting he created a culture that allowed for some marginal tactics and encouraged corruption to take root. Small lies turn into small cracks, which turn into gaping holes that swallow businesses, governments, and great people.

Trust Test - Vision

Question:

Can I use Cooperative Entrepreneurship to create the future?

☐ NO. Thank you for being honest! Consider working to refine your thoughts maybe with some peers? We will be here when you are ready.

☐ YES. Great, your next step is a BIG one!

Step #3: Take Some Risks

Question:

How do I get started?

The best way to show commitment in this environment is to take some risks. The word entrepreneurship is associated with risk. It's the answer many give when asked, "What is an entrepreneur? Answer: A risk taker." When queried about what prevents most people from living the dream of owning their own business, they respond with statements like: "I'm afraid of the potential loss," or "I can't take that kind of risk, the timing is not right."

I believe this type of thinking was trained into us from an early age. Consider that when you were a child, what was the last thing your mom said to you when you went to catch the bus? Probably something like, "Have a great day sweetheart. I love you. BE CAREFUL." The last thing you heard on your way into the big world was to *be careful*. The world is a big, scary place, and she surely did not want you to take any risks, but reality demands you take risks all time. In fact, the only way to grow as a person is to take some reasonable risks. So, assuming the child is mature enough to know what reasonable risk is, I have a new mantra for moms and dads when they send their children off into the world, "Have a great day sweetheart, I love you. DON'T FORGET, TAKE SOME RISKS."

What kind of man would live where there is no daring? I don't believe in taking foolish chances, but nothing can be accomplished without taking any chance at all.

- Charles Augustus Lindbergh

You must do the same thing if you want to try Cooperative Entrepreneurship. You have to take some risk. It is the leader's responsibility to create an environment that rewards risk taking, people who put it on the line, to tell the truth, to do something different, to be original. We're losing that willingness to take risk in American culture. We're starting to play it safe; we're allowing the government to take care of us. Take a risk, do something different. Collaborate with your associates, with other companies, and with your vendors to make a safe environment to share ideas. Take some risks . . . please take some risks. It's what will keep America leading the world.

Cooperative Entrepreneurship allows more risk taking. The group will take risks that an individual might not take by themselves. It provides a safety net for when things go wrong. The knowledge and experience of the group provides a better chance of success. It's a powerful environment in which to take risks, failing and learning, and trying again.

> Our family business took the risk to do what felt right for us and in the process created something totally original. If we hadn't taken that risk this book could never have been written.
>
> -Todd Welch

In Cooperative Entrepreneurship, we use the concept of *failing faster*. Failure is not looked upon as wrong; rather, you need to fail faster to succeed sooner. Failure is an expected outcome and the goal is to learn and progress.

> Failure is not fatal.
> - Don Shula

The world needs leaders to step up now. People that understand the culture of Cooperative Entrepreneurship, and from a gut level *they get that* :

- takes hundreds or even thousands of ideas to create an innovation.

- is collaboration of the many that will go farther than the control of an individual.

- is a vision with integrity that inspires people to give their best.

- is the rate of change that that makes Cooperative Entrepreneurship a competitive tool.

- takes modeling, measurements, and rewards to develop trusted behavior.

- is *trust* that allows all this to happen.

Completing the previous Trust Tests may have been easy for you. It's not all that unusual to find leaders who are doing the hard work to stay in their personal integrity and in turn, creating a trust-based culture around them. This next step, however, is one you may never have faced before: collaborating with your suppliers, vendors, peer companies, and even competitors to build a Cooperative Entrepreneurship Alliance.

This collaborative step still feels very unnatural to most organizations; it goes against traditional views. Fears of someone stealing your secret sauce, or a supplier taking advantage of your openess, are hard to set aside. But with experience, Cooperative Entrepreneurs learn that ceding some control and certainty will create much greater opportunties. What feels uncomfortable today will be the norm in the future. Sometimes a leader of Cooperative Entrepreneurship has to let go of control instead of trying to command more control.

Trust Test - CE Alliance (CEA)

Question:

Can you embrace Cooperative Entrepreneurship as your leadership style?

☐ **NO**. Thank you for being honest. Maybe it will fit you in the future, we will be here!

☐ **YES.** OK now your ready for the final chapter.

In the next chapter, I'll share with you the exciting possibilities the future holds as more and more people adopt Cooperative Entrepreneurship.

Lessons Learned:

1. Need is good.
2. CE Leadership is a choice.
3. CE Leaders start with honest purpose.
4. We have to balance our self interest with the greater good.
5. CE Leaders create visons.
6. CE Leaders takes risks.
7. Sometimes you have to let go of the past to get to the future.
8. Fail Faster to succeed sooner.
9. Don't buy pink Flamingos or cheap sneakers.
10. If you boss orders figs order something else.

Future of it 8

Question:

What is the meaning of life?

Not too long ago, I had the habit of asking people, "What is the meaning of life?" This, of course, amused me because no one really knows the answer. I was willing to take the risk of annoying some people with the hope of finding an original thought. I did get some very interesting answers, but only one stuck in my mind. It came from my then-13-year-old son, Kevin.

We were at the Contemporary Resort at Disney World having a snack by the pool. Kevin had sat down, and I thought to try out my question on him. So I asked him, "Kevin, What is the meaning of life?" He stopped eating his food and looked me in the eyes. It really took me aback, because I realized he was going to give me an answer. He had my full attention. Then he said, "Don't you know?" I said, "No, I don't think I do." His reply was in a tone of voice that suggested he was disappointed I had not learned this at my age. He said, "Life is about learning and having fun." He then went back to eating his sandwich, and the subject was dropped. I was stunned, not only at the clarity of his thought, but the confidence in which he delivered it. I thought to myself that this is the best answer I've ever heard.

Of courses learning can be very hard work and at times painful so I am glad he mentioned the fun part. In telling the story to my brother, Glen said he agreed with Kevin, and added one more thought to the meaning of life. He said it's also about, "Giving back." To me, those words complete what Cooperative Entrepreneurship is all about. It's about learning, it's about having fun, and it's about giving back.

Question:

What does the future look like?

Each year, some of the world's premier young entrepreneurs gather for a six week symposium at Lehigh University's Iacocca Institute. The Institute was founded by Lee Iacocca along with the Global Village Program. His vision was to bring together future global entrepreneurs with existing business executives so they can learn from each other. Does this sound familiar?

Led by Dick Brandt, it's the only program like this in the United States. It's very difficult to explain just how good the program is without experiencing what they do. However if you joined them on the first night, you would be awash in all the diversity of colors, shapes, sizes, and dialects of this eclectic group of people. In this environment, no matter how hard you try, you can't hold on to your prejudices. Everybody here is different. You meet one amazing person after another, some from country's you may never have heard of. Everyone here is also the same. They are here to learn and to teach and they share the entrepreneurial spirit of making the world a better place.

Dick shared with me a moving story of Arab and Israeli students that attended his program. Based on cultural norms, they did not engage with or speak to each other. Over the course of the program, they spent enough time together to find they liked each other and at the end found friendship. They found a way to see through cultural differences and chose to judge each other on character. Dick has a picture of them on his desk with their arms around each other on their final day.

These young people are collaborating and inventing tomorrow's world. They work together, debate, laugh, learn, and when it's time to go back to their countries these future global business leaders shed a few tears. Of course they cry, who would want to leave a community like this? Maybe the better question is, why can't we all live in this kind of business community?

Question:

If not now, when?

There is no better time then right now. In fact time is running out. We have issues that need resolution now. Who is going to do it? We are! When are we going to do it? Right now! To get there, we must reach out beyond normal business relationships to build trusted alliances with those that share our values. We must reach out to the next generation, asking them to join us, they have the most at stake. As this happens, you'll begin to get a glimpse of the future, a future that from my view looks pretty spectacular.

I don't know how long it will take to get there but there will be a time where the most valued people in our society will be those that have invested in their own personal integrity. It will have the side benefit of casting light on the dark corners of corruption. It's something we can see only by standing on the shoulders of those who have come before us and like them we are now expected to lay the foundation for the future. The only security we have is hard work and that is what it will take to make it reality. So lets get started because now is the time.

> To whom much is given, much is expected

I leave you with this story . . .

Pins and Posters

It's 1996 Summer Olympics in Atlanta, Georgia. The gold medal round of the men's soccer tournament is scheduled to start. It's early evening, humid and hot. Tens of thousands of people are entering the arena. Kiosks that sell Olympic venue pin souvenirs are everywhere, and as you look around, you see people wearing the pins on their hats and shirts, signifying their favorite sport or country. Over several days, my family and I had acquired quite a few of these little trinkets.

I'm with my wife and our boys, who were only nine and seven. We're making our way into the venue when I notice a gang of young teenage boys, somewhat scrappy and scruffy looking, approaching a kiosk; I get the distinct impression that one is intent on stealing some of these pins. I move my family around him to stay away from the forthcoming "bad news."

As we move away from them, a thought occurs to me: We have plenty of these pins on our hats and shirts so why not just share some of them? I take several pins from my shirt and hat walk towards the boy and reach over with my hand closed towards the young man. Startled, he moved back as if he thought I was going to hurt him. As I open my hand, he spots the pins and looks up at my eyes. I look back at him exchanging no words. Again I move my hand towards him, and he reaches toward me, taking the pins. We acknowledge each other again, never saying a word, as he turns and fades back into the crowd. I grab my kids and start walking into the arena.

A few moments later, just as we enter the park, I feel a tug on the back of my shirt. I turn around and there's the young man. This time he has what looks to be a stick about three feet long. I recoil, thinking he means to hit me. Instead of trying to hit me, he tries to give me the stick.

I look at his eyes, and he looks back at me. I reach out and take it. What looked like a stick I then realize is a rolled-up poster. We exchange silent acknowledgements, but again, never a word is spoken. He fades back into the crowd, I look at the poster, and I think to myself: "He felt the need to give me something back."

As I looked around, I realized that many other people had a very similar looking poster in their hands, too. They must have been passing them out for free, and it dawned on me that this was probably the only thing that this young man had to give. He gave me what he could, all he had. For a few moments, trust was created between two human beings. Now we just need to increase the numbers.

It is that simple...

-- Todd Welch

Thank you for taking the time to experience my story and I would like to learn about yours. If you're interested in continuing the conversation please join me at TrustTour.com.

The difference one word can make.

I used dictation software to speed the writing of this book. It's amazing to watch the words appear on the screen as you talk into the microphone. Sometimes the computer and I did not communicate well resulting in some good laughs. Towards the end of my writing it dawned on me to save these out-takes so you could enjoy them with me. Here are the worlds first "author bloopers." I hope they give you a good laugh.

"What will sustain you through the learning curve will be in knowing that this process will improve the quality of your life and make you a *bitter* business person." (better)

"*Clobber* Entrepreneurship is a way of thinking, it's a belief system." (Cooperative)

"When you have a club of *whopper* entrepreneurs, you can take the whole group down with you. That's why we're serious about trust." (cooperative)

"It will be your role to *confuse* the organization with tools and ideas that will model Cooperative Entrepreneurship." (infuse)

"We talked a lot about *fink*, team and trust" (think)

"It is critical for the nurturing a culture of *urination*,"(innovation)

"This is capped off with 300 years of history, *Martians* settled here among the rolling hills, two rivers, hiking, and great places to eat." (Moravians)

"This is where you want to have some real competence in the team. We decided *pure torture* was our best option. We went through a list of people."(peer pressure)

"Integrity vulnerability can *snot* only hurt you, your family and your business, but it can spread to others on the team." (not)

"And to me, that completes what Cooperative Entrepreneurship is all about, it's about learning, it's about having fun, and it's about *getting* back." (giving)

Acknowledgements

Cooperative Entrepreneurship is a living body of knowledge that is ever growing. I want to acknowledge the *teachers* I have met along the journey.

Thank you to my roots

Scott Welch So much of this book has been written about my Dad that I am concerned that if I write anymore, he will become greater than life. He is my Dad and my hero, an entrepreneur's entrepreneur who gives more than he gets. All of the work in this book is built off of the values that he has lived. We owe him a great debt of gratitude for setting the cornerstone of the philosophy of Cooperative Entrepreneurship.

Henrietta Welch On the other hand, not much has been said about Mom. She is the unsung hero. Can you imagine living with a family that is entrepreneurial 24/7? When is it family time? When do we get to be people enjoying each other? Do we have to always be creating? The funny thing is, we get the creative gene from mom, she is the most creative of us all and had a great experience being an entrepreneur herself. She has been, and still is, the rock of the family. Without her, Dad could have never have accomplished what he did. It was the combined team of Henrietta and Scott that truly created this family culture that turned into the Think, Team, and Trust culture of Cooperative Entrepreneurship. Thanks mom, I love you.

Glen Welch This book should have been co-written by Todd and Glen Welch. The only reason that didn't happen is because Glen Welch is busy keeping Charter Partners running, giving me the luxury to write about it. Glen is my partner every step of the way. Without him, Charter Partners would not exist. He is the brains behind the concepts. He is the doer behind the ideas. A lot of people have ideas; it's the few that can bring them to life that are key. Few people can say they have a partner from the moment they are born until the day they graduate. I am lucky to say Glen is that person for me.

Jody Welch As visitors have come and gone over the years, a consistent opinion has emerged about Jody: "Jody is the brightest of the group. Why don't you have her working with you?" Sadly, we've never been able to consistently attract Jody into the business. She is pursuing her passion of developing children. But she is never far away when there are key choices to be made, and we are thankful to have her as our advisor.

Jill "Genie" Gonzales, Director of Chaos, who has brought so many of my dreams to life. Jill lived this book, she has been the bridge from me to you, taking many of my raw thoughts and making them fluid. She walked me through every concept in this book, sometimes over and over again until we got them right. I hope that everyone experiences the commitment of someone who cares that much. Instead of being frustrated with my insanity she had the patience to help me find my genius (big assumption here). What do you say to someone who does that for you? The English language is all too limited… all I can say here is, thank you Jill!

Thank you to the team at Charter Partners

I work with the most dedicated and capable people imaginable. Some have been with us "forever" and all act like one big family, caring and concerned about each other and our membership.

To Pattie Cowley, Vice President and Treasurer, who has a never-ending capacity to work tirelessly and ensure our success. Pattie also has the most amazing ability to bring humor to everything, even at the worst of times. To Suzie Stark, Director of Insurance Operations, a sincere thank you for all the years of late nights, dealing with audits, pushing for on-time delivery, and for your quiet wisdom. To Frank Biamonte, Vice President (retired), who brought a perspective to the company that created clarity and balance.

The Charter Partners Associates - Everything I wrote about here comes down to what you do and say. You are the people that make it real. Thank you for living these ideas and making it possible for other's to do the same. I want thank Bill, Chris, Dawn, Janine, Kim, Johnna, and Yvette and the many people who have given the gift of themselves, in the past, to create this great organization.

Thank you, Charter Partners Members

You make all of this possible. Thank you for giving us the honor of serving you. I am especially thankful to the people who helped shape the organization in the early years:

Thank you, Charter Partners Institute.

To be a teacher is one of the greatest professions. The people at the Institute volunteer their time to teach Cooperative Entrepreneurship and they tell me it is a great honor to do it. I know that it requires sacrifice and want to thank those who have made that sacrifice including the board of directors, adult and student mentors, and the students who took the risk to try something new.

Thank you, Friends and Colleagues.

Wes Scott, Tracy Gaudet, M.D., Kevin and Chris Wolfe, all which I have known since childhood. As kids we played and philosophized and as adults we're blessed to be able to do the same thing. Thanks also to Charles Baier who co-created the "soulful lunch," we have been meeting every six months for 15 years. I have many blessing and one is to have had great coaches along the way: Jeff Vacha, Mike Oates, Mark Glat, Ed Lundeen, and Kristen & Tate Monroe.

Robert Oliver III, who illustrated this book. You have the patience of a saint and the skill to take an ambiguous concept and turn it into a simple illustration.

Britt Raybould, who edited this book. Thank you for cleaning me up and making me presentable!

Most of all thank you, family.

Our family is entrepreneurial and that sometimes means encroaching on family time. It has taken a big effort to learn about trust and then to write about it Thank you seems an inadequate acknowledgement of time that was sacrificed.

To my life partner and best friend, Kathleen. You know me the best, and you have seen the worst of me, yet bring out the best in me. You know how imperfect I am, yet I have always felt loved, that is a great blessing. Much of what I have learned about trust comes from our relationship. Without that support, I doubt this book would have ever been written. Let's keep doing "it."

To my sons, Adam and Kevin, having children is one of the great experiences of my life. As a father, your hope is that you can help improve the quality of life for your children. Of course you'll probably never read these words (who reads their Dad's book). By the way, thanks for keeping me humble all these years. It's strange to me that whenever I decide I will be "the teacher" I end up being the student again. I feel that way about being an author, too. You have taught me many things, but it is the laughter in our house that has always been the brightest moment for me.

Adam, your positive outlook, and amazing focus will take you far. Kevin, your strong will and quick wit, will carry you through life's adventures. I believe in both of you. This book is written for you as much as anyone else. I hope someday you will pass "it" on to the next generation.

Love,
Me

Made in the USA
Charleston, SC
06 December 2009

About the Authors

Todd Welch I have devoted my life to exploring trust. Along with my brother and father we have tested our philosophies in many hundreds of businesses and with thousands of students. We call our method Cooperative Entrepreneurship. With this book I share this philosophy with you so together we might make a difference in our world.

Robert Porter Lynch has helped thousands of organizations through his work on strategic alliances and collaborative innovation. He is the author of several books and has consulted worldwide He has the unique ability to create "human architecture" that can help bring more synergy to our lives and our work, i.e. the Trust Scale. I have had the opportunity to spend enough time with Robert to truly appreciate the work he is doing. His focus today is building tools to nurture honor, trust, and integrity in the world. We can look forward to seeing some new innovations from Robert.